Live Well Spend Less

Easy Ways To Save Money In Every Part Of Your Life

Sophie Gray

16
EasyRead Large

RHYW

Copyright Page from the Original Book

A RANDOM HOUSE BOOK published by Random House New Zealand
18 Poland Road, Glenfield, Auckland, New Zealand

For more information about our titles go to www.randomhouse.co.nz

A catalogue record for this book is available from the National Library of New Zealand

Random House New Zealand is part of the Random House Group
New York London Sydney Delhi Johannesburg

First published 2009

ISBN 978 1 86979 160 5

Design: Sharon Grace
Cover design: Sarah Laing
Printed in China through Bookbuilders

TABLE OF CONTENTS

INTRODUCTION	i
Chapter 1: MANAGING YOUR MONEY	1
Chapter 2: EAT WELL, SPEND LESS	24
Chapter 3: OUTDOORS	62
Chapter 4: IS YOUR HOME LEAKING MONEY?	93
Chapter 5: ROOM TO RENT	108
Chapter 6: CLEAN UP YOUR ACT	125
Chapter 7: WHEN THE RUBBER HITS THE ROAD	141
Chapter 8: OUT AND ABOUT ON THE CHEAP	156
Chapter 9: CELEBRATE WITH STYLE	165
Chapter 10: FAMILY LIFE	191
CONCLUSION	207

INTRODUCTION

I like to think we are an average household—two adults, two kids, pets, living in the suburbs ... so this is a book for the average person looking to spend less. You could probably save yourself hundreds of bucks a year by making your own loo paper, but you won't find the recipe here cos I don't want to live like that. However, if I can save some money around the house (or make some) so we can pay off a debt or save for a treat, I'm all for that.

Whether you just want to tighten your belt while you ride out a tough financial time, or make serious savings over the long term, use this book to track your progress, find fresh motivation, and keep yourself on target to achieve your goals.

Many people can rein in their spending for a week or two but undo their good work the next month, as they've made no significant changes to how they spend.

So how can you save when you are already stretched financially? *Live Well Spend Less* is a collection of easy strategies for saving money in every area of your life. Having personally lived through some very tough financial times, both as a single person and as our family has grown, I am proof that these strategies work. We've never gone without anything that was actually important, and we've achieved more than we ever imagined was possible with a low income.

I'm not going to go into a lengthy debate about the relative merits of various mortgage repayment plans or insurance adjustments, as this is a practical, pushup-your-sleeves book. Just simple ways to save money in every area of your life—so you can get on with living well and spending less.

Many people can rein in their spending for a week or two but undo their good work the next month, as they've made no significant changes to how they spend.

Let's be honest

This book is intended as a practical guide to the many simple, easy ways you can save money in your everyday life. Most of it is drawn from my own experiences, firstly as a debt-ridden and irresponsible twenty-something needing to sort my act out, and later as a young family with a fledgling business, a mortgage and a grocery budget of $50 a week.

Having been in debt myself, and experienced the pain and shame that goes with being the person who has just had the power cut off, or doesn't know if they've got enough gas in the fuel tank to get them home, a debt-free life is something that I feel strongly about. I've also experienced the enormous satisfaction of getting out of debt, seeing the savings account filling up, and knowing that the bills are paid and the holiday is possible. When we launched our first home-based business I was determined that we would endeavour to live within our means. Money was very tight but we learnt a whole bunch of really useful and easy ways to enjoy life and save money in the process.

We all have different reasons why we want or need to spend less. Some will be circumstantial, such as study time, retirement, the breakdown of a relationship, an accident or perhaps illness. Others are lifestyle choices, like ours—to run a small business from home rather than pursuing more highly paid careers. They also include dropping from two incomes to one to raise a family, 'downscaling' by taking an easier job, moving to a smaller town to destress, leaving a regular job to launch a new career or deciding to study rather than work. Some people may want to live more simply because they just want to use less of the world's resources. Others have greedily shopped, eaten and drunk themselves into debt. That was the catalyst for my first foray into a 'live well on less' lifestyle change in my early twenties. It's the truth and I had to face up to it.

Whatever your reasons for rationalising your spending, if you are new to trying to make a dollar out of 50 cents there are some challenges ahead. They're common to all of us, and to get through them, you need to keep your eyes fixed on your goals.

Goal-setting isn't just meaningless 'motivation speak'. It's absolutely essential if you want to make progress. An ambiguous ideal of dialling back the spending will not get you very far, I'm afraid. Serious savings require a strategic approach. Small, consistent savings in all sorts of areas can make a big difference to a debt without having a significant impact on your quality of life.

Goal-setting isn't just meaningless 'motivation speak'. It's absolutely essential if you want to make progress.

We try to spend less, and waste less, so we have money for the things that are really important to us. That includes paying our bills.

So what are you spending less for? If you aren't sure, check out the list below or jot down your own ideas. Putting it in writing gets it 'out there'; it helps clarify your thinking and gives you a visual reminder of what you are aiming for. Stick your list of goals on the fridge or the dashboard of the car, tape it to your credit card or save it as your screen saver.

Spending less is a little like running up the down escalator. The gravitational pull operating in society these days is to spend, spend, spend. Pay off one card with another, borrow to the hilt and hope for the best.

Eventually you just can't borrow any more, and interest payments overtake your earning ability. But the pressure to have more and better stuff never goes away. So you have to steel yourself to go against the flow. That's why being clear about your goals is so important—without that you'll lose your motivation and drift into needless spending in no time.

So what do you want to achieve?

You'll have your own goals, but here are some common ones:

- A debt-free degree
- Specific debt reduction—credit, loans, hire purchase
- Overseas travel
- Home ownership
- Lifestyle advancement—holidays, renovation, gadgets and toys...
- Single-income living for parenting purposes
- Lifestyle adjustment following retirement, redundancy, illness or other reasons

Make your goals specific, e.g.:

1. Pay off credit card by June.
2. Save $2500 for trip.
3. Not borrow any $.

Once you have written down a goal or two you'll need to set some objectives, attainable steps that take you towards your goal in small, manageable and encouraging bites.

Here are some objectives that might be applicable to your desired goal:

- Set a weekly budget so we don't end up using credit to pay for necessities.

- Pay all my outstanding fees by April.
- Reduce grocery spending by $50 per week and save the difference in a hands-off account.
- Plan to transfer $500 into fixed-term savings as soon as it accumulates.
- Put a deposit on a trip/flat/house.

Now you have an achievable objective, it's time to talk strategy.

Some cost savings are one-off decisions that when calculated over the long haul can save you loads—adjusting your mortgage repayments so you pay more on a weekly basis but shorten your mortgage term by years is one example. I'm not going to go into that stuff here as it only applies to home owners, and there are some great websites and comprehensive books around specifically on home ownership and finance.

Other cost savings are annual or seasonal things you can do around your home that reduce your cost of living, such as insulating your house, looking at how you heat or cool it, food production and transport. Some are monthly, such as the way you manage your household expenditure, family activities and entertainment.

The lion's share of your potential savings are in the weekly, and in some cases daily, decisions you will make to *not* spend on this or that, so you have money left for the things that are really important to you.

It's your choice

The harsh reality is that for most of us it's not possible to have everything we want. It is quite possible to have everything you need, though, and to have what is most important to you. It all boils down to choices.

The exciting thing is that making good financial choices is empowering, gratifying, and oddly pleasing.

Instead of feeling ground down or overwhelmed by financial burdens, you can expect to feel excited and optimistic about the future and your financial security. People write to us regularly, literally brimming with pleasure and pride in their ability to change their spending habits. It's pretty cool knowing exactly what your financial status is and that you don't have to worry. It's also not that common these days.

Living on less doesn't have to be odious and miserable—we want to enjoy life, and that's one of our goals. When you see every good choice you make actually bringing you closer to achieving what you really want, little sacrifices can make you feel really good—you can see that the choice you make to refrain from one thing brings you closer to the thing you really want.

If you ferociously pursue your goals you will be amazed at how a little can go a long way when you make a conscious decision to live well and spend less.

Chapter 1

MANAGING YOUR MONEY

Budget is a bit of a dirty word, and I have to admit that I avoid using it if possible because it seems to have negative connotations for many people. If I talked about 'budget cooking' no one would want to buy my recipe books, despite all the delicious and inexpensive dishes they contain. Instead we talk about 'fashionable food that doesn't cost a fortune', just to avoid the 'B' word.

But a budget is simply a way of organising your spending so that you can live within your means and achieve your goals. It's a tool, not a punishment for the sins of overspending.

There is no way of avoiding it when it comes to managing your money, though. Without a budget you are like a ship with no rudder. You'll drift into dangerous waters and probably sink.

A budget is simply a way of organising your spending so that you can live within your means and achieve your goals. It's a tool, not a punishment for the sins of overspending.

There are lots of ways to organise your personal or household budget, and many of them are free, using spreadsheets or online calculators. They really are fantastically clever and detailed. We use one of the systems on www.sorted.org.nz for our general household budgets. We've also created budgets for the kids (in the hope they might avoid some of our youthful mistakes). They even have specialist budget planners on there for students, and other specific variations. All you have to do is key in your details, and you can update or change the elements whenever you want so it's always current. If you get a pay rise, for example, or your hours at work are reduced, you can just change the figures in that section of your plan and it will recalculate your whole budget for you to accommodate the adjustments. It's clever stuff, it's free, and if you have internet access there is no excuse not to do it.

The less money you have, the more you need to be able to account for every last dollar. Knowing that the bills are covered and you have money allocated for your other expenses is a terrific stress-buster and gives you choices you didn't have before.

If you don't have a budget you will end up fretting about bills, feel that you shouldn't spend anything on yourself, feel miserable, treat yourself so you'll cheer up, worry about what you have spent, then fret about the bills...

FYI

In a British study into the effects of 'debt advice', participants who were in debt were asked to indicate how easy or difficult it was to carry on living a normal life while experiencing their current debt problems. The researchers used a scale from 0 to 10, where 0 was 'not at all' and 10 was 'extremely' difficult. The mean was 8.4.

Eighty-nine per cent of clients also reported worrying about their money problems 'most' or 'all' of the time. Perhaps as a consequence, the great majority of them believed their health had been adversely affected by their debt problems. Forty-eight per cent described the impact of their money problems on their health as 'great', and 43 per cent felt that their health had suffered 'to some extent'. Around three in five clients reported having received treatment, medication or counselling as a result. On average, GPs were reported to have been visited once a month, and a number of people reported visiting hospitals, counsellors or psychiatric nurses.

Relationships were also affected by debt problems. Forty-five per cent of clients stated that money problems had a negative effect on their relationships with partners. Negative impacts on relationships with children, other family members and friends were also regularly reported. In addition, 19 per cent (42 per cent of clients currently in work) reported that they had needed to take time off work as a result of money worries, and 12 per cent suggested problems led to them giving up jobs. Six per cent stated that their financial situation had led to them losing their job. Nineteen per cent reported that money problems had resulted in their finding it difficult to obtain new jobs. Finally, 15 per cent reported working longer hours to ease financial pressures.

Data also indicated that debt problems can have an adverse impact on people's health, personal relationships, housing and economic circumstances and confidence.

—*Impact of Debt Advice Research Project,* Department for Constitutional Affairs, UK, 2004

The less money you have, the more you need to be able to account for every last dollar.

If you've never operated a budget before, I personally think you can't beat a cash system. The primary reason is that cash is visible, tangible, and we don't like to part with it!

Researchers have found that people who shop with cash spend up to 20 per cent less than people who use plastic. That's reason enough alone to use a cash budgeting system.

The easiest and most flexible is the envelope system. There are variations to the way the system operates, but this is the way we found worked best with our very limited resources.

How to set up the 'envelope system'

This system is really easy to set up and operate. It's been around a long time and it works whether you are a one-person household or a large family.

I recommend using a weekly system as it's easier to keep track of—and to correct if you've run amok in the January sales.

To start with you need to know what your total annual income is, so list your income from all sources and total it. Check your last tax return for sources of income you may have forgotten, then write down the after-tax total.

Now think about your expenses.

We will divide them into two categories: **fixed expenses** and **variable expenses.**

Fixed expenses are things you have to pay every month, like rent or mortgage payments, loan payments, insurance premiums, regular transport costs, rates, and utilities such as water, power and gas. While some of the amounts vary a little from month to month (power, for example) they are predictable and you always have to pay for them.

Variable expenses are all the other things you spend money on—groceries, entertainment, sports, vehicles, personal grooming, etc.—things where your choices make a big difference to the overall amount you spend.

Fixed expenses include:

- Housing—rent/board/mortgage
- Household insurance
- Car insurance
- Medical insurance
- Life insurance
- Council fees such as rates, water rates or other local taxes
- Transport
- Utilities

Variable expenses include:

- Vehicle maintenance/servicing
- School fees and expenses such as uniforms, stationery and trips
- Sports subscriptions
- Satellite or Sky TV
- Groceries
- Haircuts
- Lawn and garden services
- Gifts: Easter, Christmas, birthdays, Mother's and Father's Day, friends...
- Childcare/babysitting

- Outings and entertainment
- Holidays
- Maintenance and repairs
- Decorating
- Clothing
- Pocket money
- Doctors' and dentists' visits
- Charitable giving, tithes, child sponsorships and donations

Include anything else that you are likely to spend money on, such as green fees, gym memberships, and magazine or newspaper subscriptions. Be ruthlessly honest—there is no point in pretending you won't buy candy bars on the way to work; you might as well factor them in so you can enjoy them guilt-free (except for the calories, that is).

Some of these expenses will be easy to calculate by looking at previous bank statements and the like. For others, such as haircutting, transport, groceries and gifts, you may have to take an educated guess—it's likely you will underestimate, so be generous in your estimates.

Deduct the total of your **fixed expenses** (mortgage/rent, insurances, utilities, etc.) from your income. The figure that remains is how much you have left for all your **variable expenses** and for **savings.**

Now you want to break it down so it's easier to keep track of. If you divide your annual totals by 12, this will give you monthly budget figures; dividing by 26 gives you fortnightly figures. I prefer to work weekly, so I divide my income and expenditure totals by 52.

If you have a surplus (more income than expenditure) you should allocate the difference to savings, as you don't actually 'need' it to get by from week to week. If the money doesn't get moved into a savings account you will just fritter it away. But you'll be amazed how even a small surplus like $30 a week will add up—over 12 months that's $1560. That's a nice little holiday or a new appliance paid for.

If your expenses exceed your income, it's time to take stock of your variable expenses and make some cutbacks. Identify exactly how much you are overspending each week, and work out where you can make cutbacks or generate extra income. This may be just a short-term situation while you clear a debt. If you have a serious shortfall you will need to look at ways of increasing your income as well as decreasing your expenditure.

Need to cut back now? Check out Chapter 2, 'Eat well, spend less', and get serious about saving at the supermarket.

- Can you reduce your spending on grooming? I taught myself to cut the family's hair, and estimate conservatively that I have saved us at least $520 per year, allowing for haircuts approximately every six weeks. That's $7800 over 15 years. A $35 haircut kit with clippers, scissors etc. got me going, and I did some research at the library and online so I could give everyone an 'as good as a bought one' cut. You could attend a night class for a small fee, and save thousands if you have a big family.

- Can you reduce your spending on garden and household maintenance? A lawn mower can pay for itself in one year—but only if you have someone in the family who will actually get outside and push it around the lawns. Having paid for the mower, can you or one of the family top up the coffers by mowing the neighbours' lawns too?
- Do you actually need those extra pay TV channels?
- Can you rethink your entertainment and outings? A coffee out every other day adds up to over $700 per year. If your expenses outweigh your income you simply can't afford this.
- Could you rent out the spare room to clear the debt while you get your spending under control? See Chapter 5, 'Room to rent', to explore these options.

How to get your envelope system working for you

The first thing you need to do is ensure all your bills are paid each week before anything else—that's a huge worry taken away immediately. Set up automatic banking payments for all your fixed expenses. For all your variable expenses you are going to use cash.

You will need to buy a pack of plain envelopes and allocate one envelope to each variable expense. Write the name of the expense and the amount you need to set aside each week on the envelope.

For example:

Groceries—$180 (9x$20 notes)

Babysitting—$10 (2x$5 notes)

Gifts—$25 (5x$5 notes)

Pocket money—$10 (1x$5, 1x$1, and 2x$2=$6 Ruby, $4 James)

Chapter 2, 'Eat well, spend less', has specific strategies for reducing and managing grocery spending. You can either include your groceries in your envelope system or use the method described in Chapter 2, or a combination of both, which is what we do. I draw the cash we need for our groceries each week and keep it in the envelope. I then follow the destitute gourmet principles for grocery spending, and any money I save from the groceries goes in an envelope marked 'Grocery Surplus'.

Once a week you will need to go to the bank and draw your envelope money in cash, in the right denominations for each envelope. I keep a card in my wallet so I know exactly how many twenties, tens, fives and coins I need to withdraw. It will be the same each week (allowing for the odd adjustment). The bank tellers have got to know me over the years; I just explain that this system works and get on with it.

If you don't have any of the smaller denominations when you need them your whole system can come unstuck. For example, if you need to give the kids their pocket money but you only have 20-dollar bills, or you need to pay the babysitter $25 and you have no fives—arghh.

Set up automatic banking payments for all your fixed expenses. For all your variable expenses you are going to use cash.

By drawing the exact denominations, you will have exactly what you need when you need to pay a bill, or pay the lawn guy, babysitter or buy a gift—the money will be there in the envelope.

If you are contemplating a trip to the movies and the 'Entertainment' envelope is empty you have to rethink your plans. No, you cannot snitch it out of one of the other envelopes, because then you won't have enough in that one when you need it. If the money isn't there you have to accept the reality—you can't afford it this week. It's not a grey area or a judgement call—the money is there, or it isn't.

If you haven't spent anything on decorating or doctors, for example, and the envelope has filled up, you can reallocate those funds—put them in your savings account or into another area where you may be regularly falling short. If you end up with an expensive dentist's bill and you need to pay it now, you can take money out of envelopes that are for luxuries like entertainment, outings or babysitting.

Bills always have to come before luxuries. It does take discipline, but if you stick with it, the envelope system works.

It works! It works! It works!

Making any purchase, whether it's clothing or groceries or gifts, will be less stressful because anytime you shop you know exactly how much, or how little, you have to spend.

We always try to allow some grown-up pocket money too if the budget allows, so buying a coffee or a magazine comes from our own 'pocket money'. We don't have to have each other's permission or justify how we spend our own money. Often that too mounts up, and it can be used for a more substantial treat, so we don't feel deprived.

You don't accumulate any interest on the envelope money as it's not in the bank, but for people with limited resources the amount of interest would be negligible anyway. And avoiding paying interest on overdrafts or loans is a real benefit.

If you are saving some money in the bank, then your savings account will be gaining interest.

You may also be worried about the security of having cash in the house. Be sensible! Don't tell teenagers, visitors or guests where you keep it. Don't put it under the mattress, in the dresser drawer or bedside cabinet. Find an accessible but unlikely spot. They're only envelopes, after all, not likely to attract a lot of attention from burglars looking for big-ticket items.

Teaching the young 'uns about money

As parents we don't want to burden our kids with worries or adult responsibilities before their time, but financial intelligence is an essential life skill. I don't believe a child will be screwed up for life if from time to time their parent says, 'No, we can't afford that', or 'We would have to save for a very long time for that', or 'We have to be careful about our spending as we need to be sure we've paid all our bills'.

The sooner they learn that the cashflow machine isn't making new money for you whenever you insert your card the better.

Pocket money

Pocket money is a good starting point. In any family there are things you must do simply because you are part of the family—helping when asked, putting away your clothes, doing dishes, etc. Those kinds of things are just part of life, and the kids shouldn't expect to be paid for simply doing their share.

Generally, children learn their attitudes towards money from home. Pocket money creates the opportunity to teach children about spending thoughtfully, saving, and the consequences of losing money, gambling with it or giving it all away.

Pocket money also helps teach children about having to make choices, saving up and waiting for things they want. Letting your children make a few mistakes is part of the learning process, and you can put limits on what they spend their money on or how much of it they can spend on lollies or junk food. (They'll cry, 'But it's MY money'; we reply, 'Only because we give it to you!')

Your child learns a lot by watching you and how you deal with money. Spending, saving, withdrawing or donating money: they're all chances to teach your child more of the basics around money.

FYI

Young people have more discretionary money at their disposal than any other sector of society. With a part-time job and regular pocket money, they can afford to have quite expensive tastes. That's all very well while they're living at home, but once they're on their own and having to pay for everything those expensive habits can be a real problem. It's hard for them to give up things they're accustomed to, like a comfortable home with a well-stocked fridge at their disposal, and a cashflow card to buy whatever they fancy.

The current generation of youth don't seem inclined to 'rough it'. KIPPERS—the acronym stands for 'kids in parents' pockets, eroding retirement savings'—are an increasingly common phenomenon these days.

What happens is this: they leave home, want all the comforts of home, spend up large, get into debt and have to move back home to their old bedroom with the Boyzone posters on the wall. Where they sponge off Mum and Dad who, God bless them, started out with nothing, used two saw-horses and an old door as a dining table for the first three years they were married, never bought anything unless they had the cash, and have worked and saved their whole lives looking forward to a retirement now being eroded by their feckless kids.

Any pocket money system you institute must be appropriate for the ages of the kids and sustainable in the overall household budget. There are lots of variations, including:

- Make pocket money totally task-oriented by paying per job: $2 for cleaning the car, $10 for mowing the lawns ... This can get complicated as they will tend to zero in on the particular jobs that yield the best return for the least effort, and may expect to be paid for doing something that didn't need doing, or do a really rubbish job and then expect you to cough up the full whack.
- Paying all the children exactly the same amount, on a weekly or monthly basis.

- Paying them to do certain tasks, such as mowing lawns, folding washing, putting out the recycling. This system can come unstuck when the child would rather go without the money than do the job but the job still has to be done.
- Pay each child according to his or her age; so the four-year-old gets $4 and the six-year-old gets $6...
- Have a linked pay scale in five-year increments—5–10 years, $5; 10–15 years, $15.

It's a really good idea to have them save a portion of their pocket money each week in a piggy bank or savings account. Kids need to experience the satisfaction of seeing money accumulate. If you give it to them in cash, with no restrictions, they are likely to spend it all every time.

Spending is one of the rewards of working and should be enjoyed, but if you want to instil sensible financial habits in the kids, then create a system so they can't spend everything they earn. Encourage them to have a savings goal—something pricey that they want to buy for themselves, so the saving has a purpose.

Teenagers and bulk funding

When a child begins college, the serious business of learning to manage their money really starts. In our family we use a system we refer to as 'bulk funding' to ease the kids into managing their money in a broader sense. Different families do it different ways, but this is how bulk funding works in our family.

The year they start college we stop paying them pocket money, and instead we allocate a sum of money at the beginning of the year for their expenses. Each month we deposit their 'allowance' into their account.

That money is to be used by them to pay for all their clothing (excluding uniforms), personal grooming and entertainment. It will be slightly less than they are likely to need so a part-time job is essential.

We pay ALL school expenses and ALL sporting or education-related costs such as camps, music lessons and tutoring. We pay all medical bills and the costs of family activities. We also pay for personal items purchased as part of our routine grocery shop—shampoo, deodorant, etc. If they want a flash, expensive brand, they have to pay for it themselves.

Some families pay the kids one lump sum for the year—if they blow it all on designer clothes in the first month they have to live with the consequences. Other families do it quarterly, which allows four chances to correct an overspend. We've opted for monthly, and that's working for us.

Some families charge their bulk-funded teens a family tax, so they contribute to family events such as holidays—making the whole thing as much like real life as possible but in a safe, guided way.

You may want to draw up a contract that outlines the obligations and expectations of each party. You might include things like 'a reasonable standard of dress and personal hygiene is maintained'; for example, boys, we have observed, will forgo replacing needed items of underwear and regular haircuts in favour of spending the money on entertainment.

While they live under your roof, you should expect them to maintain certain agreed standards, while allowing freedom of expression and personal style.

> Our experiences with bulk funding have shown that initially they are very careful with the budget. After a while, however, we found we were frequently being asked to advance money. After going through the transaction statements and seeing how much was being frittered away on drinks, donuts and other non-essentials, we withdrew the cashflow card for a while until things got back on track. Bulk funding in our house is a privilege, and you must prove that you can be responsible with money to be allowed that independence.
>
> At first, with clothing I insisted the tags stayed on till I'd seen the garment—not to control what they'd spent, just to check it was age-appropriate.
>
> I did from time to time suggest something was not a great choice, for whatever reason, and left it at that. I was surprised that on several occasions the garment was returned or exchanged!

Girls seem to make gift-giving a priority, and will allow for it in their budget or be very extravagant with gifts. In our experience boys tend to opt out of gift-giving, having spent all their money on other things. We don't think this is on, and believe they should be giving too, as they'll be there with their hands out every birthday and Christmas. Check out Chapter 9, 'Celebrations', for easy, inexpensive gift ideas that they can try.

FYI

Theft and standover tactics

Cellphones and cashflow cards carry risks—standover tactics or outright theft must be discussed. One teen we know received a text from the phone of a mate, telling him to meet him at a certain place. When he arrived there he was held up at knifepoint by a stranger who, having stolen the cellphone, was working his way through the contacts list, sending texts to arrange meetings with all the kids, who assumed the text was from their mate simply because it came from his phone. After forcing them to the cashflow machine he extracted all their money. Fortunately for our friend, when it happened to him he only had 11 cents in his account! (No surprises there, but it could have been much worse.)

What to do in a financial emergency

With the best intentions in the world you may face financial hardship that requires external help.

- The first thing to do is contact your creditors and explain the situation—see if you can set up a payment plan.
- Can you take a 'mortgage holiday' or 'insurance holiday'—this means your provider allows you to miss or delay a payment without it affecting the terms of your agreement. You will have to arrange this with them and establish the exact terms of the break. You cannot simply skip a payment and call it a payment holiday—they will see it as defaulting on your payments. Nor are they obliged to grant a payment holiday, but if you are a longstanding client with a good payment history it is worth asking.
- If you have several outstanding debts, such as hire-purchase agreements, credit cards and personal loans, identify which has the highest interest rate and pay that off first.
- If you have a personal loan with a lower rate than the other things, consider paying off all the others using the loan, and then chip away at that over time, paying the lesser interest rate.
- AVOID AVOID AVOID borrowing from 'fast cash now' money lenders. The terms and interest rates are crippling. What may seem like a quick solution

to your problems is likely to make a bad situation much worse.

- Contact a budget advisor—www.familybudgeting.org.nz is the website for the New Zealand Federation of Budget Services. You can use the site to find free budget advisors in your area. Alternatively, look in the phone book for Budget Advisory Services—this is a voluntary organisation with branches in most areas.
- Talk to Work and Income or other social services—they may be able to offer suggestions.

Budget Advisory Services and the Citizens Advice Bureau are **free** services. Citizens Advice Bureau, www.cab.org.nz, can provide information to assist with almost any issue, and if they can't, they'll find someone who can. Whether you're about to be evicted from your flat, need to find local childcare, or want advice on how to deal with a neighbour, they have trained CAB volunteers to assist you. They'll discuss your options with you and give you contact numbers for any services or organisations that will be able to help further.

Emergency food

If you are unable to buy groceries and are ineligible for emergency funds from the government social services agencies, then a food bank may be able to help you.

Food banks are generally run by churches, and staffed by volunteers. Their stock comes from donations.

Don't be embarrassed to ask for help—that's what the food bank is for. They will probably want to know how many people are in your household, and you may need to explain the cause of your hardship. Organisations vary—some food banks will supply fresh food and meat as well as staples; others only supply tinned and shelf-stable items.

They may well have a limit on how many food parcels they are willing to supply to any given household, and they do not usually give more than one per week as they do get exploited. Some will allow several deliveries but require you to take budgeting help or other advice or training.

You are not obliged to attend their church, and accepting a food parcel should not put you under any feelings of obligation. Most churches provide a food bank because they simply want to help. The Salvation Army and Presbyterian Support Services are nationwide 'ministries', but many local churches take responsibility for trying to meet the needs in their communities and will take referrals from Work and Income or other social services and community trusts.

If calling a food bank makes you squirm, but you have no food, think of something you can offer in return—then you may feel more comfortable receiving the assistance. Can you, for example, offer to do some cleaning or mow a lawn, or deliver a letterbox drop by way of thanks. You can also make a contribution to the food bank when you are back on top of your finances.

Chapter 2

EAT WELL, SPEND LESS

Like most households, our fortunes have ebbed and flowed over the years; career moves, the advent of babies and general changes in the economy have all affected our ability to generate and manage our income.

When our first baby arrived we experienced 'income shock' as we adjusted to living on one income instead of two. Then we started our own business, Rich surrendered his salary and company car, and income shock hit us again. Overnight we became a 'low-income household', watching every penny and discovering how hard it is to live on less when you've never had to before. With determination and a bit of native cunning we adapted to our circumstances and learnt to live well, but we discovered all the common pitfalls of low-income living along the way.

This chapter holds many of the keys to the success of living well on less. It is also probably the easiest for anyone to implement and begin to see results. More cash in your hand, better food on the table and a greater sense of wellbeing are all direct results of applying the strategies outlined in the following pages.

Living well on less and staying out of debt is liberating and empowering because it means you do have some control over your circumstances, whatever your situation. It's a much more comfortable place to be than constantly teetering on the brink of a cashflow crisis.

Nowadays we're experts at pulling in our horns and tightening our belts through tough financial times, and we have learnt a lot along the way.

- We know that drifting around the mall window-shopping makes you feel dissatisfied and jealous, and often leads to unintended spending. As the proverb says, 'What the eye doesn't see, the heart doesn't grieve over'.
- We've learned to take advantage of specials or sales only when we have a surplus. Little economies make a big difference in the long term.
- We've learned that our kids would rather have parents who are happy, relaxed and able to play and spend time with them, than parents who are worked ragged, or worried sick because we can't afford to pay off some unnecessary bit of knick-knackery that seemed like a good idea at the time.
- We've learned that the best things in life really are free.

We are fortunate in that we have chosen our circumstances, but for many people illness, redundancy, marital breakdown, accident, bereavement or even the need to study means there are no choices. They find themselves struggling to cope on a low income, and many fall victim to what I refer to as the '3 Ds'.

The 3 Ds stand for Depression, Debt and Divorce.

So how do the 3 Ds affect you?

When someone finds themselves in an 'income shock' situation, or they are struggling just to manage from one day to the next on a low or reduced income, it's common to feel miserable at times. And that's not surprising; when you are unable to have and do things that you are accustomed to, or that everyone else you know takes for granted, life can feel extremely unfair. After all, you are just as deserving as everyone else; you may even be working harder than everyone else! You may also be coming to terms with the cause of the change in your circumstances. That in itself can be traumatic—an accident, illness or relationship breakdown doesn't leave a lot of emotional energy for making good financial choices—and all too often the result is Depression.

Those feelings of depression, if not dealt with, can lead subtly but steadily to the second D—Debt.

It's natural to want to comfort and reward yourself when you feel low. Or simply to have what everyone else is having—cake with your coffee, a weekend away, a smarter vehicle...

It's easy and cheap to amuse yourself by browsing auction websites on your computer at home or drifting around a shopping mall on a rainy day. The trouble is that you inevitably see things that you desire.

Shopping malls and supermarkets in particular are designed specifically to make you want to spend. Every few days new stock arrives, so that what you have, or what you are wearing, quickly seems out of date or is superseded by a new model or a different style.

Sale and 'Special Offer' advertising is everywhere, chipping away at your resolve, and tempting and encouraging you to buy. It has nothing to do with need—it plays on our emotions, our wants and desires.

If you can't afford it, nothing you buy on sale is a bargain when it ends up on your credit card and you are paying interest on it.

Comfort shopping can very quickly become a source of tension and stress—you didn't intend to buy anything, and you knew you couldn't afford it, but you bought it anyway. Now you feel guilty, and you worry about the cost—or shout at the one who spent when they shouldn't have, making you both feel miserable. The pressure piles up as the bills come in, exacerbating the feelings of depression and shame, and over time the stress erodes the fabric of your relationships.

It's easy to see why the third D stands for Divorce. Frustration, sickness, depression, anger, blame and shame are the most common culprits when financial stress causes a relationship to break down.

Financial pressure is frequently cited as a significant factor in relationship breakdowns. My advice is: if you want to look after your relationships, don't get into debt. If you are already in debt, use the strategies in this book to pay it off. Take control.

While the 3 Ds affect all areas of domestic money management, they're particularly relevant when it comes to groceries and food shopping. This is because grocery spending is one of the biggest variable expenses in any household (flip back to Chapter 1 for a definition of fixed and variable expenses).

FYI

A British study into the broad effects of debt advice found that, at the extreme, debt could result in relationships being 'messed up' and could cause separation. Interviewees also described their debt problem as having a very negative impact on their relationships with children.

They also frequently spoke of feeling guilty about the financial restrictions imposed by their debts. For instance, parents were unable to pay for the leisure activities or material possessions their children were accustomed to. School trips, clubs, holidays and new clothing were among the examples cited.

Problem debt proved to be a very isolating experience. Interviewees described losing touch with friends, as they could not afford to go out socially. This could exacerbate feelings of stress. In addition, aside from general stress and anxiety, feelings of guilt and loss of self-esteem, interviewees sometimes described quite severe emotional health problems, as well as physical problems, such as eczema.

—*Impact of Debt Advice Research Project,* Department for Constitutional Affairs, UK, 2004

Because you have to do grocery shopping so frequently, it's the area in which you are most likely to 'blow out' the budget regularly. The weekly grocery shop is also probably the area where you can potentially save the most week in and week out.

Food is also an emotional issue—it's one of life's greatest pleasures. Food is fundamental to the way we celebrate; we also comfort and reward ourselves with food (some of us a little too much, it's fair to say).

The weekly grocery shop doesn't just include food, though—nowadays we are also bombarded with new product ranges in the supermarket aisles every week, with everything from flat-screen TVs to outdoor furniture on sale alongside the milk and bread. The subtle message is that these things are also necessary, just as the milk and bread are necessary—after all, the supermarket or grocery store is where we go to buy our essentials.

Most people tell us they aim to be in and out of the supermarket in around 45 minutes or less if they can manage it. So if you need to buy on average around 30 items (the number *Consumer* magazine uses as the model for an average shop when they do their supermarket price comparisons) that's an awful lot of decisions in a very short time. Factoring in the choice of brands and varieties, special offers and out-of-stock items, you'll have to make somewhere in the order of 205 financial decisions in 45 minutes—that's roughly one decision every 4.5 seconds:

'Where's the one I want? Oh, it's out of stock, but this one's on special—ah but that one is bigger ... maybe I should get two? Do we have any left at home? Oohh, is that my phone? Darn, missed it. What was that, sweetie? Yes, I know you need the loo but there are no customer toilets here, you'll have to hold on. Now where was I?'

And so it goes on, as we go up and down every aisle. Often we'll just put an item into the trolley because it's easier than deciding whether or not we actually need it, and we certainly don't want to 'run out' of something during the week.

There are no other regular financial decisions involving hundreds of dollars that the average householder makes in this cavalier manner. Spending $100 on a garment may involve thoughtful consideration, maybe even consultation with others, and lots of comparing—'Is this my colour?' 'Does it make me look fat?' 'Will it go with everything else I own?' 'Is it nicer than the one in the other shop?' and so on...

With grocery shopping there is a tendency to simply put all the stuff you fancy in the trolley, with little or no thought such as 'Do we need it?' 'Can we afford it?' Because it's groceries, and we want it, we just buy it regardless.

At the checkout we agree to pay large sums of money—hundreds of dollars—without a second glance. We pay using credit or cashflow cards, so there is little connection between the brain and the wallet, and we are detached from any sense of our money actually changing hands. Plus most of us are already thinking about something else before we've even left the store (in my case, I'm trying to remember where exactly I parked the car).

Many, many people then repeat this process several times in the same week without considering how much they've already spent or whether they've got value for money.

I hear people complain all the time that it's expensive to feed the family, as if they've had nothing whatsoever to do with the process. We do need to buy food, but this is a really dumb way of handling such significant expenditure. That's why I'm going to explain a much better way to go about doing it.

When the children were little I used to get together with an informal coffee group of other mums. We all had kids around the same age, and I remember how awkward and embarrassed I felt when we'd meet together in a café.

Everyone else was buying coffee and cake, and fancy little bottled drinks and treats for their kids. I had just enough money in my purse to buy a coffee, and I'd bring sandwiches and a drink from home for my littlies' snacks.

I felt like such a mean mummy—why was my child the only one who couldn't have a treat! I didn't mind so much going without something for myself, but I really did mind when I felt my kids were missing out.

I knew that I could make a whole cake for the price of one piece of café cake, and the home-made one would be nicer, and that my child was probably better off with my healthy sandwich and bottle of water than a sugary drink and snack, but I still felt rotten all the same.

One particular time a friend offered to order my coffee for me, as she was ahead in the queue. I passed her my money, she paid the cashier, and without even thinking popped my change into her purse. I needed those two small coins to make up my bus fare home! Sooo embarrassing!

Those situations ceased to be a problem when I identified that socialising at each other's houses or meeting in parks and playgrounds didn't present the same problems. A plate of home-made cake and a thermos of coffee shared at the beach was more fun for everyone, especially the children, than jamming into a crowded café. And it was a lot cheaper!

I hear people complain all the time that it's expensive to feed the family, as if they've had nothing whatsoever to do with the process.

If you want to eat well and spend less, then you need to approach grocery shopping strategically. I am going to take the whole process apart, and give you a method for dealing with each part of your shop so you only buy what you need, with the result that you have money left over at the end to spend on other important things in life.

This method has been proven over and over. In fact, we've received hundreds of letters and emails from people who have been staggered at how much they've been able to save and how it has transformed their financial outlook.

Each step is simple and easy to implement. It will cost you nothing at all to revolutionise your shopping methods, and it will save you thousands of hard-earned dollars.

The first thing is to plan the menu

For busy people who want to watch what they spend, the menu plan is an essential household management strategy. Often the hardest part of feeding everyone every day is just deciding what to make. There are either too many choices or not enough, and the last thing any of us needs at the end of the day is a hard decision.

Menu planning is the easiest way to take the stress out of the daily dinner dilemma. What have I got? What will everyone eat? How much time do I have? What happened to the meat I thought I'd defrosted?

Whether you are a single-person household, flatting, a couple or a family, the menu plan is the surest way to guarantee something not just edible but actually palatable makes it onto the plate every night. That little bit of thinking ahead can save you a bundle in last-minute takeaways and emergency dashes to the supermarket. It will also allow you to factor in or use up any stockpiles in the pantry or fridge so you have less waste.

I personally never know what I fancy for dinner, and when I ask Rich he throws it back onto me without skipping a beat, saying 'Just make something easy'. The thing is, it would be easy if he'd simply tell me what to make!

Some years back I started to get the kids writing a weekly menu plan, hoping they wouldn't complain about the dinner so often if they were the ones who had chosen it.

I asked them to select six *proper* dinners for the week, allowing one night free for socialising or something on toast. The result was a revelation.

Doing the shopping was quicker and easier because I knew exactly what I needed to buy. Budgeting for meals was straightforward, and the daily dithering in front of the open pantry while I tried to cobble together a meal at the end of the day ended altogether. (Along with a lot of the 'Yuk, I don't like this' variety of dinner-table conversation.)

I asked them to select six *proper* dinners for the week, allowing one night free for socialising or something on toast. The result was a revelation.

The menu plan is a stress-buster on so many levels. It helps you to rein in the grocery spend by reducing overstocking, and eliminates the time wasted doing expensive emergency dashes to the supermarket because you are missing a vital ingredient you were sure you already had.

The plan can accommodate supermarket specials and seasonal variations, and the dishes you choose can be selected to suit the age and stage of your household. The menu plan also makes it much easier and more achievable to cook double batches, squeeze in some baking or get a head start on the next day's meal when today's is under control.

So if you want to spend less, then get smart and plan your meals before you need them. Here's how.

Getting set up

- Eleven recipes—that's about how many the average household can manage to stock ingredients for, remember how to make, and coerce the family to eat. Households tend to shop and stock for all 11 of their regular dishes even though they are actually only going to make seven each week.
- Work out what your repertoire of 11 dishes consists of, and how much those dishes cost to make. Make a list of the dishes you eat most often, including breakfasts, lunches and snacks in the list. Then roughly work out which are your most expensive dishes and why.
- We frequently know in advance which are our busiest days—in your menu plan, prepare for those days. When we are busy, sports training, parent interviews or the late shift all conspire against us and make quick-fix meals from the supermarket or takeaway seem very appealing. Be prepared!
- Plan to include some dishes that are quick to make on those busy days, such as risotto and fresh veg, or spicy meatballs in pita bread with salad, or a stir-fry and rice. Fast food from home is much cheaper and healthier than fast food from a store or takeaway outlet.
- Alternatively, make a double batch of something the night before and use it again the following day. Or break out the slow cooker and have dinner waiting for you when you tumble in the door. This

is a great option when you have flatmates or teenagers coming and going at all sorts of different times. A big batch of soup and some rolls will give everyone a fast, filling meal dirt cheap.

Things to consider when planning your week's menu are:

- How many people are in for dinner on each day?
- What time does it need to be ready, so that people can eat before they shoot out for evening activities?
- What do we have in stock already?
- What's in season?
- What will everyone be prepared to eat? (Not what do they like—if we only ate what we actually liked I personally would subsist on potato crisps, cake, and fillet of beef.)

When you have a rough outline of the kinds of dishes you intend to make, look at the overall menu:

- How many meat meals are there?
- Can you afford those dishes?
- Are you including a wide variety of foods?

Review the menu plan regularly:

- Are there small changes you can make that will save you money?
- Can you replace one family favourite with another that is less expensive?
- Can you use a cheaper cut of meat or make it go further by adding extra veg?

Decide what kind of plan will work best for your household—you can plan a weekly, fortnightly or monthly menu.

Think about what is in season, what is on special, and what special events you need to factor in (e.g. entertaining, sleepovers, birthdays). Your menu plan can be as simple as dinners for every night of the week, or it can go as far as including all meals and snacks.

In our house we don't plan all our food to that degree, as it would make me feel like I was following a diet (horrors!). But some people, particularly those with large or very busy households, find it a real stress-buster. Some households just rotate the same menu week in and week out; if this works for you, and doesn't bore you senseless, then the fewer decisions you have to make the better.

Other things to consider:

- Take into account what day is your regular shopping day—it's likely that the day before shopping day you will be getting low on fresh produce so factor that in—a stir-fry might not be possible but cottage pie with veg from the freezer might.
- Choose main-course meals with the cost of the key ingredients in mind, rather than out of habit.
- Reduce your reliance on ready-made kids' meals. If you are feeding babies and toddlers, choose recipes that can be served puréed for baby or chopped for toddlers, as well as appealing to

adults. Leftovers can then be frozen and used for kids' meals when you are having something that's unsuitable for them.

- It's easy to assume that dinner is the most expensive meal of the day, but a household of teenagers or flatmates can hoover up an alarming amount of Coco Pops and fancy toast over a week of breakfasts. Cornflakes, Ricies, Weet-Bix and rolled oats are economical choices for every day: keep treat cereals as treats.
- Lunches, snacks and prepackaged bars can cost loads, and drinks—juice, fizzy, coffee, wine and beer—all slip down without drawing a lot of attention.
- You may find that regularly 'adjusting' the menu subtly is the way to go. Split fancy cereal with a cheaper brand, or only have it once a week and let the porridge and Weet-Bix make a comeback; maybe save the juice and fizzy for weekends.
- A few minutes spent spreading stuff on slices of bread for the lunchbox, rather than snatching a few packets of snacks, will make a big difference to the grocery budget within a couple of months.

Having a menu plan means everyone knows what they can have when. Stick it up where everyone can see it.

Record what you spend each week, and determine which week's menus were the tastiest, healthiest and most economical, then if you want to take it a step further you can combine them to create a master menu.

Doing the shopping

My destitute gourmet method for managing your supermarket spending is based on three principles which will save you money, improve the nutritional quality of your meals and ensure that they are also delicious. It is derived from our own experience, and incorporates some tricks of the trade that I learnt working in restaurant kitchens.

The principles work because it is not like following a diet—each household has different tastes and needs, and the principles form a framework on which you fill in the details, allowing you to choose the things that are most important to your individual household. They'll help you discern the difference between a need and a want, and allow for treats and special occasions too. Sticking to these principles can save you thousands of dollars a year, and it's easy.

The three 'dg' principles are: **Shop smart; Eat healthily and in season; Make a little of something luxurious go a long way.** These three principles can be applied to any household or budget, freeing up cash for other important things in life like debt reduction, education, holidays or handbags.

Before you begin you need to establish what you are currently spending on groceries. Look up your bank or credit card statements for the last month and write down how much was spent on groceries—not just in the 'big shop', but including any other smaller trips where you may have picked up one or two items. Total them up to get the true figure for your week's grocery expenditure—yup, takeaways too, as they are a food expense.

dg principle No.1. Shop smart

Make a list of all your basic 'pantry essentials'

These are all the things you need to have in stock to keep the family ticking over—not what you LIKE, just what you NEED.

The essentials list should start with fresh fruit and veg. I discovered very early on that I could make a wider variety of nourishing meals by combining fresh produce with basics that I already had to hand in my pantry, such as flour, rice, eggs and seasonings, than by using canned or frozen veg. Those things do have their place, but with fresh produce you get more for your money, and you can do more with it—provided you buy what is in season. You may need to consult a 'seasonal availability calendar' to familiarise yourself with what is in season at various times. More on the seasonal stuff later.

It wasn't always exciting, when money was very tight; we ate a lot of vege soup, vege curry, vege frittata, vege pizza, vege samosas, vege fritters, apple crumble ... etc. But it was tasty, nourishing, filling and healthy.

Under 'Fresh Fruit and Veg' on your list note down basics like onions, garlic, potatoes, carrots, apples—whatever you consider the basics, taking into account seasonal variations.

Next you are going to list your basic range of staples—things like flour, bread, eggs, milk, butter, oil, baking powder, salt, dried pasta ... Just the basics that YOU use regularly. Not what you think you might use if you ever get around to dusting off that recipe book ... YOUR pantry staples.

Next you will write down a basic range of cereals—actually, this is a basic range; copy it: Cornflakes, Weet-Bix, Ricies, rolled oats. If your household likes anything more exciting than that, there's a different list you can write the treat cereals on later.

Add to your essentials list a basic range of canned foods, then a basic range of seasonings, sauces and spreads. Then you can include a basic range of frozen food—remember, it's just the essentials—peas and beans are fine, ice cream and frozen pizza? They're going on that other list.

The essentials list looks quite different from one household to another, as age, life stage and personal taste obviously differ hugely.

After you've listed all your essential food items you need to add meat, and then essential cleaning products. You may want to read Chapter 6, 'Clean up your act', before you do this. Cleanies should take note that while different sprays for every room of the house and little dingly-danglies for the loo are nice, they are not necessary. Just the essentials. Then list essential toiletry items and pet supplies.

Essentials list

This is what your essentials list might look like:

- Fresh fruit and veg—onions (red? brown?), potatoes, carrots, garlic, apples, bananas, what is cheap and in season at present ... write them all down
- Staples—flour (plain? self-raising? wholemeal?), oil, sugar, eggs, milk, butter or spread, baking powder, salt, cheese, lentils, rice (long grain? sushi? Arborio?), macaroni...
- Baking stuff—coconut, vanilla, raisins, cocoa, yeast...
- Spreads—peanut butter, honey, jam, marmalade, Marmite...
- Cereals—Cornflakes, Weet-Bix, Ricies, rolled oats
- Canned food—baked beans, tinned tomatoes, chilli beans, kidney beans, sweetcorn, tuna, peaches...
- Sauces—tomato sauce, sweet chilli sauce, soy sauce, Worcestershire sauce...

- Frozen food—peas, beans, mixed veg, pastry sheets...
- Seasonings—mixed herbs, oregano, cumin, curry powder, coriander, mixed spice, cinnamon, Mexican seasoning, basil...
- Meat—beef mince, pork mince, boneless chicken breast, bacon...
- Cleaning products—fly spray, bleach, floor cleaner, surface scrub...
- Toiletries—loo rolls, shampoo, conditioner, soap, shaving cream, razors, sanitary products, hair-spray...
- Pet supplies—cat food, fish food, flea treatment...

Your essentials should include the basic components of your regular meals. It should also include baking basics, and in some cases there may be things that you regard as essentials now but if circumstances changed they could be omitted from the list. I use an asterisk to mark items that may not always be considered essential—chocolate, salami and ham, any store-bought beverages, including wine ... If we are in a tight spot, these are not essential; when we can afford to have them I would include them in my regular shopping.

When we were living at our most frugal—four people and a grocery budget of $50 per week—we had a very meagre range of essentials but we never ever went hungry. There was always something I could make from the 'essentials'—a bowl of porridge for breakfast, a batch of scones for lunch, a pot of soup, vegetable pizza or a simple curry.

Once you have made your essentials list, it's time for that other list. I call it the 'luxuries' list.

Make a list of luxuries

On this list you are going to write anything your household likes, but is not essential to your survival—ice cream, wine, fancy cereals, little dangly things to hang in the loo, biscuits, packet meals, fancy oils, kids' foods like nuggets or lunchbox bars...

These lists are really important—it's impossible to differentiate between a need and a want in the 4.5 seconds of thinking time you have in the supermarket aisle. What the lists do is establish quite clearly the priorities, and put some boundaries around what we buy.

Instead of saying, 'We have to watch what we spend, so there will be no treats for the foreseeable future', we identify that a little treat is important to avoid a big blow-out later on. Otherwise it's like living on a diet—it won't work long term.

Old-school housekeeping

Back in the 'olden days' husbands gave their wives housekeeping money. It was a finite sum from which they had to manage the household expenses, pay bills, buy groceries, replace school shoes, etc. If Mum blew the housekeeping on a new Dior coat there might not be any new shoes for the winter. A household's quality of life was substantially influenced by how well Mum managed the housekeeping. If she was canny and careful, and Dad's vege garden did well, then there might be a family holiday or new TV on the horizon.

These days, with credit cards and cashflow machines, it's easy, very easy, to continue to spend long after the money has all gone. While I don't want to don a housecoat and curlers and ask my husband for money, I do appreciate that putting a limit on what you can actually spend on groceries, or 'housekeeping', to use the old term, is sound economic sense. This is how we do it.

Draw your grocery money in cash

So, you have now established what you actually, really, honestly spend at the supermarket and food suppliers, and have regained consciousness. You need each week to draw that amount of money in cash—yes, I know it's a lot!

Only shop once a week

If you are serious about saving money you need to decide that you will only go to the supermarket **once** a week.

If you think you can pop in for two minutes and buy one thing, you are deluded. You'll be in the supermarket for 20 minutes and you'll probably buy five or six things. They make sure you do. There are literally dozens of subtle strategies operating at any one time to get you to part with the 'maximum spend' while you are in there. It's not wrong—it's good business. Everything from the layout to the lighting has been considered in terms of its impact on you spending your money while you're in there.

If you want to leave the supermarket with some money left over to spend on the other important stuff in life then you need some strategies of your own. And the first is only going to the shop once a week.

If you run out of something, go without or make do till the following week, you'll be amazed at what you can manage. You will use up all the old cans of bean salad in the back of the pantry, and learn to use the ingredients you bought for a special recipe you never got around to. Necessity is the mother of invention.

My PA told me recently about a string of cooking disasters one evening that led to the development of what her kids now call 'favourite dinner'. The sauce from one failed recipe, the rice from another and the only veg left in the house, slung together in a desperate attempt to salvage something from a culinary crisis, and the result was the creation of 'favourite dinner'! Admittedly, it's not Mum or Dad's favourite dinner, but boy, it's cheap to make, quick, easy, healthy and her kids love it. Imagine if she'd just given up and bought takeaways. They'd never have had 'favourite dinner' in their lives.

Avoiding the emergency dash to the supermarket and takeaway will save you hundreds and hundreds of dollars. Over a few weeks you will get to know how many litres of milk you go through in a week, how many loaves of bread, how much loo paper and how long the laundry powder lasts. So you will not be over- or understocked. Use your essentials list to note how many of certain things you need to buy, or how frequently you purchase bleach or oil, for example.

Avoid semi-prepared products and ready meals

It's expensive to eat ready-prepared meals, and nutritionally they have severe limitations. Home-made food tastes better and is better for you, but young people's palates in particular have become very conditioned to the flavours and textures of processed foods.

If spending less on groceries is a priority for you, then decide now not to buy anything you can realistically make yourself. Many people are surprised when they realise how much they depend on convenience foods, and have assumed ready-made foods are available because they are difficult or time-consuming to make at home.

While that's true of some specialised items, much convenience food is simple everyday stuff—pasta sauces, gravies and seasoning mixes, salsas, dips and pastes, pizzas and soups, vegetable gratins, baked goods and breads—all bottled, bagged, boxed, snap-frozen, tetra-packed and canned for our convenience.

So why bother making a recipe from scratch?

Home-made food is more flexible than ready-made, leftovers can be frozen, ingredients substituted and improvisations made to accommodate specific dietary needs. Seasonings can be adjusted to cater for individual likes and dislikes. Recipes can be adapted to maximise ingredients that are in plentiful supply, with the added bonus that the home-made version will often be cheaper, have superior flavour and nutritional value, and contain no additives, preservatives or ingredients you can't pronounce.

There are some brilliant convenience foods—tinned tomatoes, baked beans, tinned sweetcorn, stock, tomato paste and basic frozen veg—and I wouldn't be without them, as they are inexpensive and versatile. Just be selective.

In deciding not to buy anything you can realistically make yourself, it's important to accept that what is realistic for one household may not be realistic for another. Similarly, you might be able to manage more 'from scratch' cooking in a few months as you've had more experience, or less because you've had triplets!

Pasta sauces, pizza, casserole seasonings, biscuits, muffins, curries, muesli, lunchbox bars, Mexican meals, sushi, Asian stir-fry type meals, etc. are all readily available in semi-prepared or takeaway forms. But the home-made versions are easy to prepare, much cheaper, and generally much better tasting, depending on the recipe of course. And they're usually a lot healthier as they will have lower fat and salt content than processed food, more vegetables and no preservatives.

Just doing some baking is a good place to start—two or three easy, 'makes a lot' recipes for muffins and biscuits can save you heaps. It doesn't take long, and they taste so much better. If you don't have any recipes ask friends—they'll give you their tried and tested ones, and troubleshoot for you if you don't know one end of an egg from the other.

Cooking is not a 'gift' or 'talent' you have to be born with. It's just a practical skill, like driving or reading or tying your shoelaces. The more you do it, the better you get at it and the more it makes sense.

Keep a price book

Alphabetise a notebook and write in all the products you usually buy and their prices. The price book enables you to accurately determine when something is on special (supermarkets often put little labels up which imply that the price has been adjusted even if it hasn't).

When competing supermarket mailers come through the letterbox you can choose where to shop. You can price your grocery shop before you do it, even cost out your favourite recipes using your price book.

You can even draw up a table in the back, note down your week's recipes from the menu plan and tally up what you spend on groceries that week. So you can establish which were your least expensive weeks and why.

Your shopping list

If you are only going to shop once a week you need to take a good list with you. Write your shopping list with your menu plan, essentials list and luxuries list in front of you.

- Check the menu plan: Monday—honey pork stir-fry.
- Check the essentials list: do I have the veg I need? Fresh, frozen?
- Do I have the staples I need: noodles, oil, soy sauce, honey...?
- Do I have the meat I need? Can I substitute something I already have?
- Am I including a luxury or treat this day? Nah, it's Monday—harden up.

And so on through the menu plan. Then check your essentials list for other staples such as butter, cheese, spreads, baking needs and so on.

Choose one or two luxuries—only if you can afford them—and check your cleaning products.

You should have drawn the grocery money in cash, as discussed earlier. If so, armed with cash and your list you are ready to do the supermarket shopping. If something is not on the list then you don't need it—even if it's on special, you don't need it. You never even thought of it till you saw it on the shelf with its bright 'Special Offer' label. Remember, you made all the decisions before you got to the supermarket. Don't even go down aisles if you don't need anything from them. Don't browse; you will inevitably see things you want if you go looking.

Shop around

In the supermarket

Buy the supermarket's own brands—house brands can save you lots of money. When there are several quality levels on offer I use the basic range for staples like flour, milk, etc. and the supermarket's 'named' range for most other items. You may need to experiment a bit—we are still not converted to house-brand baked beans, but I haven't bought a bag of branded flour in years!

Fresh produce

The supermarket is rarely the best-value place to buy meat and fresh produce. Find a local supplier for these items.

People often ask me if it's really worth going to several shops for groceries—by the time you've used the extra fuel and time surely it's cheaper to buy everything in the supermarket? I have done costings on this, and the savings are substantial.

For example, I can save $137 per year just buying my spuds from my greengrocer, not to mention carrots, onions, apples, mandarins, lettuce, tomatoes and bananas, etc.... all of which are cheaper in the greengrocer.

Those hundreds of dollars will pay for more than a little fuel. The savings add up to a family holiday!

Meat

Meat is even easier to cost-compare, as it's not so affected by seasonal availability and we tend to stick to a range of cuts that the family likes and that fits our menu plans. Simply compare the price of lean beef mince and boneless chicken breast in your supermarket with the price offered by a wholesale butcher. The difference is significant, and if you have freezer space and have planned your menus, you won't have to go every week.

Is the price on the sticker the only price? Many butchers will give a discount for bulk purchases. A bulk purchase could be anything upwards of 4kg. It's worth asking, especially if you have space in the freezer.

Meat makes up a significant chunk of the average grocery bill. The following tips will ensure you are getting the best for your buck:

- Review what cuts of meat you purchase regularly and whether they are appropriate for your budget. We don't eat steaks and fillets—they're too pricey—but we enjoy delicious casseroles, beef and burgundy pies, and rich, spicy chillies and curries, all of which use inexpensive cuts of meat so we can afford to add a splosh of wine or other little bits of luxury.

- Go for quality over quantity. I don't buy cheap, nasty meat to save money. I buy the best we can afford even if it means we have less.
- Where do you buy your meat? I love the convenience of the supermarket but it is rarely the best-value place to buy meat and fresh produce.
- Do you know which are the cheapest cuts and which are the most expensive? Check out the 'Meat cuts' section at www.destitutegourmet.com.
- Do you know how to cook less expensive cuts of meat?
- If you are big meat consumers, consider buying a whole or half lamb, or half a beef 'beast' from your butcher. They'll cut it into the appropriate portions, including making mince and sausages, along with chops, fillets, steaks and the rest. It's a lot of meat, but the price when averaged out is MUCH cheaper than buying a bit each week. My local butcher charges roughly $6.50 per kg for beef and $8.99 per kg for lamb. If you can't use that much, consider going in with a family member and see if you can share their freezer too. Around 30 per cent of what you get will be what we would consider to be gourmet cuts—the steaks, fillets, etc. The remaining 70 per cent is useful for stewing, casseroling, etc.

Ethnic ingredients

Check out the Indian and Asian grocery suppliers in your area; many items will be substantially cheaper than in the mainstream supermarkets.

Get the household on board with your budget goals

Discuss the benefits of the choices you are making—if you need to, introduce an incentive to encourage cooperation.

Any money you save each week goes into the 'Grocery Surplus' envelope. Use this fund for bulk-buying specials, paying unexpected expenses such as doctors' bills, school trips, babysitters, gifts, debt reduction, treats ... quality-of-life stuff.

dg principle No.2. Eat healthily and in season

It's not just cheap it's delicious...

I had very little experience of cooking pulses until a vegetarian friend pointed out how much I could save by using less meat in our meals. I began to research the nutritional benefits of pulses and the way they were traditionally used in the cuisines I loved—French provincial, Mediterranean, Mexican, Italian, Indian and Asian cuisines. I found that pulses have been a staple for peasant cultures for generations, and the cuisines they developed are what we now eat in restaurants! I realised I could create those dishes at home using the same principles that the peasants did, basing the meal around a starchy carbohydrate—rice, pasta, pulses, grains, breads or noodles—which are all very cheap, and are often high in fibre and low in fat. I then bulked the meal out with seasonal vegetables and used a small amount of good-quality lean protein (because I don't want to eat cheap, fatty meat) to create really tasty meals. The seasoning, what gives the dish its identity, is often the least expensive part—a teaspoon of spice only costs about 25 cents.

Lentils, kidney beans, chickpeas and the like are very also cheap and are one of the foods nutritionists recommend we eat more of, because they are excellent sources of protein, iron and fibre and contain no fat. We use them both instead of or in addition to meat.

Instead of using eight sausages to feed four people, I could now use three really good-quality butcher's sausages, veg, plump creamy cannellini beans and tinned tomatoes, and make a delicious and much healthier cassoulet-style meal—a French peasant dish good enough for guests.

Better still, it's not just cheap and delicious, it's a really healthy way to eat.

Eat in season

It can be difficult to identify what's in season when you buy produce in the supermarket, because there are 'plums', for example, available all year round—they may have been imported at vast expense and refrigerated until they've lost all vestige of flavour, but they are there.

At your local fruit and veg shop it's likely the most plentiful foods are the ones at the peak of their season, and are therefore the cheapest and freshest.

We eat these till the seasonal banquet rolls around and something else comes into season. Eating seasonally ensures constant variety—instead of having frozen peas every night, we might be eating corn and courgettes and aubergines and tomatoes for several months, then more broccoli and cauliflower, celery, pumpkin and sprouts.

Your local fruit and veg shop should be experts in storage, so you get the freshest produce. They will also be able to tell you how best to store your purchases to minimise waste.

We use lots of seasonal vegetables in our meals. Generally, half the evening meal will be vegetables. I'm not talking about a plateful of boiled carrots and peas. We use the carbohydrate and vegetable portions of the meal to make the meat go a long way. Add extra vegetables to a family casserole and serve it in a ramekin with a cobbler topping, or in a pasty, or wrap it in a flatbread or crust, fill the plate with some more inexpensive seasonal produce and you'll not only extend your housekeeping money, you'll improve your health.

We borrow culinary styles and techniques, flavour combinations and seasonings from some of the best and most exciting cuisines in the world so the dishes are interesting, fashionable and delicious—they are also affordable.

Gradual changes to your household food culture are easy to introduce if you plan ahead. Swap beef burgers for bean burgers, or try bean nachos instead of mince ... It's not just cheaper, it's healthier! You'll need to have a recipe handy and the ingredients in stock to make the changes actually happen. Having the menu plan decided ahead of time makes it easy.

A glance at the menu plan also gives you a quick overview of the household's nutritional profile. How many red meat or fish meals are you eating? Are you eating any pulses? How frequently is pudding on the menu? Do your meals include sufficient servings of fruit and veg? Do you start out intending to eat one thing but actually buy takeaways?

dg principle No.3. Make a little of something luxurious go a long way

Using your 'luxuries' list

From your 'luxuries' list just choose one or two items when you do your weekly shopping—and only if you can afford it. You will find you become far more careful about how you use luxury ingredients to keep meals interesting, and you will use less. Having access to some of your favourite foods or ingredients helps you stay on track, and a little treat may prevent a major blow-out later on. The trouble is that without a list we see so many things we like (that aren't essential but are nice) we end up overspending.

Restaurants use a little bit of a luxury ingredient to 'sell' items on their menus —like 'Fettuccine with smoked salmon in a light creamy sauce'. There may only be a little bit of smoked salmon in the dish, but the use of the luxury ingredient is clever. A little bit imparts a lot of flavour, and by telling us it's in there they have led us to expect a delicious creamy smoked salmon flavour.

Home cooks often neglect the power of description.

What's for dinner?

The first chef I worked with told me that people eat with their ears, then their eyes, then their nose and lastly their mouth.

The more basic the meal, the more effort I make over presentation. Stack the corn fritters in the middle of the plate, arrange the salsa decoratively, garnish with something fresh-looking...

I remember stretching a small amount of meat by threading it on skewers interspersed with vegetables and serving them on a timbale of seasoned rice with the sauce in a little dish on each plate—it was a humble meal but my kids gasped in awe and said, 'Ooh Mummy, you made a "restronk" dinner!'

Restaurants never admit to serving leftovers, but a daily 'Specials' list is something we have come to expect when we are handed a menu. If the chef has an ingredient that needs to be used, you can expect it to feature in the Specials menu.

Make sure your diners know there are good things in there—tonight we're having a delicious home-made calzone with spicy beef, roasted vegetables and parmesan cheese in fresh yeast bread crust; i.e. last night's leftover chilli with the remaining roast pumpkin from the night before, spread onto a fresh pizza base, with a bit of parmesan grated on, then another pizza base placed on top, edges pinched together and baked—gorgeous, filling ... leftovers.

There is also no substitute for the satisfaction of leaving the shops with cash in your hand that previously would have been spent. Actual physical cash is a powerful motivator. How much you save is up to you.

How the savings work

If you have followed the strategies in this chapter, drawn your usual grocery money in cash and shopped following the 'dg principles', you will have come home with cash left over. Hooray! We call that the 'Grocery Surplus'. Find an envelope, write 'Grocery Surplus' on it, put the leftover money in it, and put it in a safe place. Under no circumstances tell teenagers where you keep it.

Each week you want to try and add to it. The money in this envelope should initially be directed at debt elimination. When you have no outstanding bills or unpaid accounts then the money that accumulates in the 'Grocery Surplus' envelope can be channelled into other areas—bulk-buying supermarket specials, for example.

This doesn't mean you revert to spending it all like you used to, though. As that money mounts up it can pay for holidays or outings, it can be directed into long-term savings or the shoes and handbags fund—it's up to you!

If you don't draw your grocery money in cash, and just apply the principles, leaving the grocery surplus in the bank account, it will disappear—I'm not sure exactly how or where it goes, it just seems to be eroded by other unconscious spending.

There is also no substitute for the satisfaction of leaving the shops with cash in your hand that previously would have been spent. Actual physical cash is a powerful motivator. How much you save is up to you.

Chapter 3

OUTDOORS

When I was growing up, my family were not 'gardeners'. In fact, my mother's approach to gardening was to do an annual purge, which I dreaded with a fierce intensity, involving as it did lots of lugging of heavy, prickly piles of stuff around, ripping out weeds and generally making ourselves useful when we could have been off playing with our friends.

The fact that anything edible ever emerged from our garden was purely an act of God. The fruiting plants produced fruit every year with no assistance whatsoever from us. Mostly the garden was for fun—splashing about in paddling pools, letting off fireworks, playing at camping, and galloping around pretending to be horses. The majority of our neighbours sacrificed their gardens and put in swimming pools. Our section remained resolutely grass, an excellent arrangement that suited everyone—we could swim in their pools and they could do handstands on our grass.

The value of the garden as an appreciating asset or a source of inexpensive food was something that few households in our street seemed to consider. Most people had a lemon tree, we had a kiwifruit vine because it just grew on the fence, and another chap had a passionfruit vine and used to spend every summer in his wheelchair guarding the vines from rampaging hordes of kids intent on stealing all his fruit. But no one had a worm bin, a compost heap or even a herb garden. Parsley and mint grew under the drippy drainpipe round the back, but basil hadn't even been invented yet.

A few decades later, owning a house is about getting onto the property ladder. Viewing your home as an appreciating asset is not a bad idea, and looking after and maintaining your assets and getting the most out of your investment is sound economic sense.

Landscaping

Statistics suggest that landscaping can improve the value of a property substantially, adding as much as 15 per cent to the value of your real estate. If your property is valued in the $200,000–$225,000 range (before landscaping), an effective home-landscaping design can add $30,000 to its value. It will also enhance your quality of life for as long as you live there (and can still leave plenty of room for handstands and fireworks). Landscaping not only creates outdoor areas that we want to be in, giving pleasure, adding value and looking after the environment, it can also save us money by providing a venue for social events and a source of food.

Statistics suggest that landscaping can improve the value of a property substantially, adding as much as 15 per cent to the value of your real estate.

As a rule of thumb, developers suggest that you should calculate on spending 5 per cent of a property's value on landscaping. But don't panic, you don't have to spend thousands or even hundreds of dollars all in one go! You can plan your landscape design, then implement it over a period of years.

Hard landscaping, walls, drainage, tree removal, etc. are all hard physical work and expensive to do, so real estate agents agree that like any type of property development, this has to be a shrewd business decision and not become just an issue of personal taste.

Before you start

Ascertain what kinds of home landscaping represent the current trends for the real estate market

Landscaping has fashion trends just like clothing, food or anything else. You may love the idea of a cottage garden and a white picket fence, but will that make your property appear dated and out of fashion, or will it provide a timeless accent to a period property? Should you include water features? Formal planting? Native plants or exotics? Heritage planting? What's the current trend in your area?

Observe what other people in your area are doing

If everyone on your street has a camellia hedge, camellias probably do well in your area, and a hedge may be a better option than a wall or fence which may not blend into the surrounding environment. Whatever you do, it must complement the style of the other properties in your street. Adding value is not about expressing your individuality, it's about doing things that will make someone else want to spend more to buy your property if you decide to sell.

Make use of magazines, books, television and the internet

These all provide an abundance of information about what kinds of home landscaping designs are currently 'selling'. By all means look for ideas and inspiration, but don't get carried away. Calculate your budget and plan a design that fits it.

Consult a professional if you can

Any time you are planning to spend a large sum of money it's worth taking advice. If you can't afford or don't want to pay for a landscape designer's advice, at least try to mine some ideas from your local nursery. You may find this advice saves you more than it costs. Plants can be pricey, and if they aren't happy where they're planted they have a nasty habit of dying. Experience and training count for a lot when it comes to knowing what will work where, how high something will grow or what the impact of planting that little climber might be on the rest of the property in years to come.

Talk to the agents

Real estate agents see the reactions of potential buyers to home landscaping day in and day out; consult them about trends, what they consider essential, what turns potential buyers off. Remember, this is not about personal taste, it's about returns on your investment—it may be that your planned water feature will yield a better return if the area is paved for parking instead.

You can design your own landscape

Library books, websites, etc. can all be helpful, particularly if you have a flat site. Bear in mind though that planting plans, propagation instructions and feeding and pruning schedules etc. may have been written for a different climate, or even a different country.

If you can find a design that suits your existing garden shape and structure you are off to a good start. If you have an unusual site then it may be difficult to get all the elements right without expert advice.

Landscape plans

A planned garden doesn't have to happen all at once. If you develop an overall plan, you can save towards and work on one or two areas at a time, leaving other areas for later in the year or even the next season or two, according to whatever your budget will allow. Resist the temptation to rush out and buy all the plants in one go. If you aren't ready to plant then they may die before you get around to using them.

Shopping around may take a little longer, but it can save you loads. You'll get the same long-term result, it just costs you less.

A landscape designer should take into account where the sun is, what your soil type is and what kind of look you are after. Once you have a plan you can start to shop around for plants, hard materials etc., and handle the planting and installation yourself. The landscape designer should bear your budget in mind when specifying plant types, but if necessary you may also be able to substitute a cheaper plant for an expensive one without ruining the plan.

A planned garden doesn't have to happen all at once. If you develop an overall plan, you can save towards and work on one or two areas at a time, leaving other areas for later in the year or even the next season or two, according to whatever your budget will allow.

Friends of ours purchased a house with an inground swimming pool at the back. The pool was in a lovely sunny spot, but was very visible to neighbouring properties. After much deliberation our frugal friends paid for a professional landscape designer to draw them a landscape design.

During the consultation they were able to discuss the various uses of the space: pets, kids hurling themselves in and out of chlorinated water, outdoor entertaining and food production.

The need for privacy was paramount, and consideration had to be given to what screening plants would be best; plants that shed lots of leaves or fronds would result in endless hours of extra work cleaning the pool.

The final plan was presented, our friends searched out sources for some of the larger plants, and the planting plan was implemented over several seasons. As a result of good design and planning, within two years the new plants had grown so much that the privacy issues had been resolved, while other areas of the garden were still being developed. Some substitutions were made—for example, a hedge of lime trees was replaced with cheaper and more practical lemon trees—without detracting from the overall plan. The landscape plan was money well spent.

Employing a landscaper

Discuss with the landscaper exactly what role you want them to play. They will agree a plan with you, but like any building project you may find costs escalating. You will need to determine who supplies what.

If you have purchased some materials already, can you source more if required? Is your landscaper prepared to shop around, or are they tied in to using particular suppliers?

Who is going to project manage the job, them or you?

Container gardening is something you can do even if you live in a small apartment or flat, and it's a brilliant and satisfying way to both save money and add variety to your meals.

We spent the first nine years of our family life in a small starter home on a shared driveway. We had our own tiny bit of lawn, which was steeply sloped, shady and damp. We did have a big, sunny deck though, and made the most of it—paddling pools, tents, birthday parties...

We were exceedingly broke at the time, so to add variety to our frugal meals I grew food plants in containers, concentrating on the flash and fancy bits that made the meal seem special—herbs, baby vegetables, fresh salad greens, berries, lemons, etc. At one time we had 11 different foods growing on the deck.

As we had NO money to spare, the first crop of tomatoes came from the seeds of a cherry tomato nicked from the salad bowl after lunch at a friend's house.

Our next house came with so much garden we hardly knew what to do with it—it even had an existing vege patch. But growing food has much less to do with space than with soil and sun. Our nice new vege patch was bereft of any nutrients and too shady!

Luckily I haven't lost the knack of container gardening, and our deck is currently home to 32 strawberry plants—growing in everything from a 'proper' garden-centre plant trough to old clay pipes that I chiselled some holes in, a collection of cracked pots and a plastic bucket.

Container gardening is something you can do even if you live in a small apartment or flat, and it's a brilliant and satisfying way to both save money and add variety to your meals.

Eating your assets

Quite apart from adding value to your property, your garden can also be used to grow food, supplementing your groceries and saving you money. Even if you know nothing about gardening to start with, you can learn. Seek out older neighbours who garden. Chances are their years of successes and failures will save you from some disappointments. They will also have some experience of what will and will not grow in your area. They may even share some of their surplus seedlings with you.

Choose your site carefully

Whether container gardening or planting in soil, ensure the area is sunny for six hours a day, and easy to access.

You'll need to be able to get water to the area (a hose can be run up onto a deck or terrace just as easily as down into the garden) and you need to have good nutritious stuff to grow the plants in. Soil goes rock hard in containers, so potting mix or compost is preferable. Vegetables planted near trees will always have to compete for sunlight, water and nutrients, and may simply lose the battle.

Even if you know nothing about gardening to start with, you can learn.

Compost bags or 'grow' bags

Grow bags are so easy and cheap to make, and they are a great solution if you have no useable ground to plant into. You'll need to buy large bags of compost, each of which will hold eight to 10 seedlings. Compost is available from nurseries, hardware stores and even the supermarket. Lay the bag down flat, and using a sharp knife poke some holes in the bottom; these allow water to drain out so your compost and plants don't rot. Then turn the bag over and cut eight to 10 crosses in the top side of the bag.

Open out each cross and make a hollow in the compost. Gently plant one seedling per opening. Water them well, and make sure you put the grow bag in a sunny spot. They'll need to be watered every day, and if it's really hot, morning and evening. Within a short time your plants will grow lush and green.

When the plants have finished fruiting, rip them out and tip the used compost into your garden. Having several compost bag gardens or 'grow bags' on the go at the same time is a cheap and convenient way to supply the kitchen with salad greens and herbs. The bag is a garden that even a very young child can maintain and take pride in. You can position the bags against a sunny wall, on the deck, on a flat roof or by the back door—anywhere you have plenty of sun. You can even have it in a wheelbarrow, so that you can wheel it out for the morning sunshine then tuck it in the garage overnight if you think there will be a frost.

Container plants

Almost any vegetable that will grow in a typical backyard garden will also do well as a container-grown plant. Vegetables that are ideally suited for growing in containers include tomatoes, peppers, eggplant, spring onions, beans, lettuce, squash, radishes and parsley. Climbing plants need to be staked or positioned near a wall or trellis so that they can scramble up it. And a hose or sprinkler handy to where you are growing will be a huge help.

Pots

Garage sales, flea markets and the like are excellent for picking up old but perfectly good containers. Even cheap plastic buckets with a few holes punched in the bottom will do. Discarded loos, sinks and baths can make quirky, longlasting planters, as will old wheelbarrows, barrels and pipes. I've even seen food plants being grown in old gumboots and teapots!

Tyres

Old tyres make great planters—they're cheap, portable, moisture-resistant and retain the heat. Select three or four tyres of the same size, stack them and fill them with compost. If you are stacking tyres more than three high it's a good idea to 'lace' them together with some wire so they can't topple over. Potatoes do particularly well in tyre gardens as you can plant in layers.

Paddling-pool planting

An old paddling pool works particularly well as a vege garden on a terrace, roof garden or rocky area. Punch holes in the bottom of a rigid plastic paddling pool, lay some scoria or gravel in the base for drainage (you don't want the drainage holes to clog up with soil or the garden will become waterlogged), then fill it with compost or soil. The pool will be deep enough for a wide range of crops, it's easy to manage and will last several years. You should be able to reach all the way into the middle from the edges, and it will be large enough to be quite productive.

Not for the birds

Birds are a constant menace to food crops. I've tried all sorts of bird-scarers, including several cats—very cute, but useless at bird-scaring. I've spent ages stringing up all the old and awful CDs only to have the wind blow them away, and I've also used netting, really difficult when you want to prune or harvest crops.

The latest and so far most successful solution has been to string up some very cheap mini-disco glitter balls, purchased from the $2 Shop. These little balls are polystyrene with tiny pieces of mirror all over them, and they're super-sparkly. The balls are lightweight, so they spin and twirl in the lightest breeze, bouncing reflective sparkles off every leaf and surface. It's a bit like some wacky art installation but the birds just don't know what to make of all the reflections so they stay away—hooray! This piece of horticulinary genius is worthy of an international award, I feel—it's easy, cheap and really works.

Great gardening ideas

Free

- Discarded woollen carpet makes excellent weed-mat. Turn the old carpet pieces 'pile' side down on the earth, and cover with landscaping bark, mulch or whatever you are using. The carpet will biodegrade slowly, reducing moisture loss from the soil and suffocating weeds at the same time. You can cut holes into it to position plants, and because it is porous, water will soak through, keeping plants and worms happy. Keep your eye out for discarded rolls of carpet—just be sure it's woollen, not synthetic.
- Old newspapers are another good free weed-mat option. Arrange a thick layer of newspapers over the area, spray lightly with the hose to stop the papers sliding or blowing around, and cover with mulch or bark.
- Gardeners are a generous lot—let people know you are after free plants and you will undoubtedly be offered some—probably clumping types of plant that need thinning every few years, as well as surplus seedlings and bedding plants. Some gardeners love to raise plants from seed, which invariably results in way more seedlings than they can use.

- Offer an exchange—a batch of baking or an afternoon helping with weeding in return for some surplus plants will probably be warmly received. If you take the 'help with the weeding' option you may also learn a lot during that time.
- Keep a look-out for landscaping crews. Replanting, whether it's a municipal flower-bed or a home garden, will result in plants being removed. Ask politely if you can have the discards or leftovers. With a little TLC you can end up with fine healthy plants, or even just one plant from which you can harvest cuttings to propagate.
- Collecting seeds—saving the seeds from the previous year's crops—costs nothing. Store the seeds in named and dated envelopes or bags, and discard any that are mouldy or moist. Do a little research before you plant them out. Some seeds need to be soaked or germinated before going into the ground, others may do better if started in pots then transferred to the ground. Seeds are terrific value.

When I first started to garden, my front neighbour, a retired gentleman called Douglas, took great pleasure in encouraging my endeavours. His garden, though not much bigger than my little postage-stamp patch, was so stunning it was featured on a gardening TV show. He had espaliered fruit trees along the fencelines and had plums, pears and almonds in profusion. His flowers fragranced the whole neighbourhood and I'd often wander down with the babies just to admire the blooms.

Douglas taught me how to grow a wide variety of plants from cuttings, and sent me off on walks to snitch bits I liked from other people's hedges and see if I could grow them. I have a white climbing rose which produces a profusion of flowers every spring that was grown from a cutting taken from another cutting two houses ago.

Not only did Douglas teach me a lot, but I'd often come home and find a bowl of plums on my doorstep—my family benefited from his surplus produce as well as his generosity of spirit. Now I'm the one with the plum trees, and the family next to us has the concrete landscape and little babies. I hope I live up to Douglas's example.

- Take cuttings—a small pot of 'rooting hormones' and a little patience can yield dozens of healthy little plants. I've grown a box hedge, loads of roses, hydrangeas and all sorts of other plants by dipping cuttings in a little liquid root stimulant and planting them out. You'll need to do lots, as not all will take, but it's the easiest way to propagate shrubs and you only need to use small cuttings. During pruning times ask neighbours if you can 'snitch' a cutting or two from what they have pruned off their plants.

- Search via the internet—gardeners with a surplus would always rather give plants away than throw them away. Look under 'Free for removal' type headings.

Cheap

- Check out local markets, fairs and car boot sales. The plants may not look as perfect as the garden centre offerings, but they'll be a lot cheaper and with a little TLC they'll thrive. My tamarillo tree cost 50 cents at a school fair and it provides us with loads of lovely tamarillos as well as being a very attractive plant.
- Ring your local council's garden work department and ask if they sell surplus trees and plants from their municipal planting projects. Because they buy in big quantities and plant thousands of plants each year, some councils are happy to sell off their surplus very reasonably. They get rid of their oversupply, generate some revenue and encourage the vegetation of the neighbourhood.
- Buy directly from the grower. Buying a quantity of plants for a landscaping project directly from the grower can be significantly cheaper than buying through a nursery. Some even deliver. You'll need to be quite specific about what you are buying, and will need to be ready when it arrives.
- Phone the landscaping companies in your area and ask what they do with surplus plants. You may be able to purchase at a wholesale rate rather than

at retail rates, or you may be able to barter for a few surplus specimens. I have found chocolate cake a surprisingly effective negotiating tool.

When we moved to our current home a section of the garden was waterlogged due to poor drainage, and absolutely jammed with water-loving weeds and wild ginger. Digging all those weeds out of the sodden soil was too big a job for us. A building company was doing major work nearby, so I entered into negotiation with a digger driver and fixed a deal with him whereby for a modest fee and a chocolate cake to share with his crew he would bring his digger over to my side of the road. Two hours later he had scooped out all the weeds, dug a deep pit, buried them so they'll never see the light of day again, created a level patch and a retaining wall so we now have a flat bit of lawn for playing on, and scooped out the stream that had blocked up and caused the drainage problem in the first place. Good manners and a bit of native cunning can go a long way when you are landscaping.

Cheap insecticide

Prevention is often the best option when it comes to insects. Make a strong solution from crushed garlic cloves and warm water. Strain into a spray bottle, add a little dishwashing detergent to help it stick, and spray onto vulnerable plants and seedlings. I use this on beans, tomatoes and pretty much everything in the salad garden.

Companion planting

There is plenty of material already written about companion planting. The principle is simple—plant something the insects don't like next to something they do. Some combinations work because of scents that repel insects, others work because they attract good bugs. Mixed planting results in a balance and diversity of plants and species that, in turn, attracts pest predators and avoids the pest-ridden effects of monoculture, which is the planting of rows and rows of the same plants. Fields of lettuce, corn and onions, for instance, are a paradise for a pest or disease that, once introduced, can simply move from plant to plant.

French marigold and calendula have been shown to be highly beneficial as companion plants. Lavender in the garden will attract bees, which will in turn help pollinate the plants, resulting in a higher yield from your crops.

Cheap plant food

Compost, made from kitchen waste (excluding meat and bones, which attract rats) and garden waste is the best possible food for your plants.

Choose a warm, sheltered site away from houses or play areas. You can make a heap or use a compost bin; either way start with a layer of coarsely chopped twiggy, woody material on bare soil or grass. Add alternate thin layers of green matter and brown matter (small twiggy, branchy stuff or straw) preferably in layers no more than 5–10cm deep. The brown layers, being twiggy, allow air to circulate as well as adding to the nutrient mix. You can add food scraps, manure, fresh grass clippings (not too much at once or it will go slimy), weeds without seeds, vegetable scraps, seaweed, tea leaves and bags, coffee grounds, torn newspaper and cardboard, egg cartons, prunings, dry leaves, bark, untreated sawdust, wood ash, twigs and sticks.

A handful of blood and bone mix will 'activate' the composting process but is not essential.

Your compost shouldn't be smelly. If it is, try adding some more green matter and forking in some grass clippings, which will heat it up and speed up the decomposition.

Composting tips

- If possible cover food scraps with a layer of grass clippings or green material to reduce fruit flies.
- If you can't be bothered layering, just make sure there is a mixture of green and brown stuff. Smaller pieces will decompose more quickly than big stuff.
- For quick compost, fibrous materials should be no bigger than the thickness of your finger.
- Avoid cat/dog/human faeces, meat, fish, bones, oil and invasive weeds.

- If you don't have a compost bin, cover the heap with a tarpaulin, plastic sheet or piece of carpet underlay; this helps keep the heat and moisture in and the neighbourhood pests out.
- The heap should be moist; if it is not, add some water—a spray from the hose will do it—and use a cover.
- Compost needs air, whether in a heap or a bin—turn it every few weeks to mix it up, aerate it and speed up decomposition.
- Once an open compost heap reaches a height of 1 metre, or the compost bin is full, it's time to start the next one. If you're using a bin, remove it from around the compost, cover the compost, and position the bin again to start the new batch. Compost can be ready in four months during warm weather and six months during winter. Well-maintained and turned, it may be ready in as little as six to eight weeks; if left entirely to its own devices it will take 12–18 months.
- Mature compost is sweet, dark and crumbly, and you shouldn't be able to recognise any of the original components.
- When it's ready, dig it into the garden. You can also use it for pot plants and for potting up seedlings.

Compost tea or compost soup

Compost tea is a nutrient-rich organic fertiliser teeming with micro-organisms. It's easy to make at home and it can be applied directly to the leaf surface of a plant as a foliar spray or used as a soil drench to improve plant root systems.

- Mix one part good, mature, well-rotted compost with six parts water in a large covered bucket and let it steep for up to 10 days. Tap water contains chlorine, which is non-selective when it kills micro-organisms, so it'll kill the good stuff along with the bad. If you let the water stand overnight before you use it, much of the chlorine will have been released, resulting in a more potent brew. Compost tea enthusiasts use all sorts of filters, bubblers and tubes to aerate and oxygenate their brews, but for a beginner this basic method is fine.
- You'll need to give it a stir every day, more than once a day if you can manage it, which helps oxygenate the mixture.
- After a week to 10 days, pour the resulting liquid through a filtering cloth like muslin or cheesecloth into another bucket or watering can. Dilute the mixture until it is the colour of tea and pour it into a watering can or clean sprayer. Compost tea can be applied at two-week intervals; leftover compost tea will get smelly and should be discarded, so use it or lose it.
- It's a good idea to start a new batch as soon as you've used the old. It will be ready 10 days later when the plants are due for their next feed.

Eating from your garden all year round

A vegetable garden will significantly reduce your grocery spending, and provide the freshest possible produce. Likewise a selection of fruit trees will ensure you have something to pick all year round for snacks, lunchboxes or dessert.

Fruit trees will take a year or two to settle into production, but imagine if you never had to buy apples, plums, mandarins, lemons, oranges or pears—the trees will pay for themselves in their first year of production, then every year after that is a bonus.

For a guide to what to plant and when to harvest, you can consult a harvest calendar: www.gardengrow.co.nz has an online kitchen-garden version divided into specific climate zones; they'll even email you reminders so you know when it's time to plant the next lot of seedlings. Using a harvest calendar increases your likelihood of success because it will be geared to your climate.

Storing your surplus

If you are growing fresh fruits and vegetables you will inevitably end up with a seasonal surplus. Home bottling and freezing are easy and cheap ways to make the most of these surpluses.

What happens when you freeze food?

Freezing involves changing the liquid content in a food to ice. It slows the process that causes food to break down, holding it in suspension and retaining the colour, flavour and nutritional content of the food. The following is a rough guide to what happens when you freeze a wide variety of foods. Sometimes you may want to freeze just the food on its own, or sometimes you will freeze your surplus as part of a recipe, and the freezing process may affect the texture of some of those foods.

- Fruits or vegetables with a high water content or a delicate cell structure do not freeze well. These include lettuce, tomatoes, watermelon, citrus fruit sections and cucumbers. Most other foods can be frozen with varying degrees of success; some foods will change in texture but are still very much useable—tomatoes and frozen capsicum halves, for example, will be soggy when defrosted but are excellent in pasta sauces, goulash, on pizzas, etc. Potato soup may be gluey when defrosted, but mashed potato on top of cottage pies is fine—go figure!
- Sauces and gravies thickened with flour or cornstarch frequently separate and break down when frozen. Modified starches that are used in commercial frozen foods are not generally available retail, so for best results freeze stock for gravy unthickened and add thickener when you reheat it.

- Cooked egg whites tend to get rubbery when you freeze them; if you want to freeze a mixture containing cooked egg white chop it finely.
- Mayonnaise breaks down when frozen so use a salad dressing instead if you are making sandwiches for freezing (jam soaks into the bread—frozen jam sandwiches are nasty).
- Cakes iced with butter icing freeze well, but icings based on whisked egg white do not.
- Milk freezes well, and so do most natural cheeses, but they may crumble more when you thaw them.
- Yoghurt may destabilise and lose its creamy texture; if so, the excess whey can be poured off or stirred in. I just freeze the yoghurt in Popsicle moulds and the kids eat it frozen; that way there are no detectable changes and surplus yoghurt doesn't go to waste.

Do I have to blanch food before freezing?

Some foods are significantly improved by blanching before freezing. In other words, pop them into boiling water for two or three minutes to arrest the enzyme activity that causes the food to ripen, then plunge them into cold water and drain. The blanched food can then be spread out on a tray to freeze. When frozen, place it in a clean bag or container and you have 'free-flow frozens'.

- Blanch vegetables such as sweetcorn, broccoli, cauliflower, carrots, peas and beans.

- Blanching is not required for foods such as berries, capsicums halved with the seeds removed, and chillies.

Can I freeze cooked vegetables?

Semi-preparing vegetables can save time and money. For example:

- Sauté mushrooms or courgettes in butter and freeze.
- Mash avocado with lemon juice to use when they are out of season and expensive.
- Sauté onions and garlic and freeze.
- Make pesto and freeze it in ice-cube trays.
- Freeze surplus tomato paste so it doesn't go to waste.
- Mash potatoes and freeze them in small mounds; use individual mounds as required to top casseroles.
- Grate fresh tomatoes when they're in season and freeze them in 400-g bags; use to replace canned chopped tomatoes.

Can I freeze fruit?

Freezing is a great way to store surplus fruit. Prepare it quickly, in small quantities. Wash the fruit in cold water a few pieces at a time to avoid bruising; an antioxidant like lemon juice or ascorbic acid dissolved in the water will help prevent discolouration. Prepare it as required for serving—stewed, sliced, mashed or whole—then pack it in appropriate serving sizes and freeze promptly. Alternatively, cover in a sugar syrup made from 1 cup of sugar to 3 cups of water and freeze the fruit in the syrup. If you are using rigid containers allow room for expansion.

You may get 'off' flavours when you use iron or chipped enamelware utensils, so it's best to use containers designed for freezer use.

What causes freezer burn?

Freezer burn is a brownish discolouration caused by moisture loss; it's not dangerous but it does make the food less appetising. To avoid freezer burn, squeeze or suck (if you are brave enough) excess air out of plastic bags and seal them tightly. If using containers, eat the food within a reasonable timeframe or freezer burn will occur on the surface.

How can I use my freezer more efficiently?

A full freezer uses less power than an empty one; pack empty space with plastic bottles filled with water—this will keep the power usage down, and it will also help keep everything frozen in the event of a power outage. A full freezer may remain frozen for two days or so; a half-full freezer will start to defrost within 24 hours. In the event of a power outage, insulating the freezer with spare blankets and quilts will trap the cold inside, slowing down the defrosting process.

How long can I keep frozen foods?

Bought frozen foods usually have an approximate storage time marked on them. If you keep meats solidly frozen they will remain safe to eat well beyond the recommended time; however, they may show quality changes like rancid off-flavours in the fats or dryness from freezer burn.

Some recommended storage times for frozen goods:

- Fruits: 12 months.
- Vegetables: 6–12 months.
- Roasts and whole poultry: 6–12 months.
- Steaks and chops: 4–6 months.
- Minced or ground meats, stewing meats: 3–4 months.
- Cured and processed meats lose quality more rapidly than fresh meats because of the presence of salts, so don't store luncheon meats, franks, ham or sausages for longer than 1 or 2 months.
- Thaw frozen meat in the fridge; thawing at room temperature gives surface bacteria a better chance to multiply.
- Baked yeast bread, scones and rolls are best used within 3 months.
- Use unbaked yeast bread dough within 1 month—unbaked dough may require more yeast than usual, as freezing will damage some yeast cells.
- Un-iced cakes also freeze well, but storage times vary. Store angel food, chiffon or sponge cake for up to 2 months; cheesecake 2–3 months; chocolate cake 4 months; fruit cake up to 12 months.

- Nuts also freeze well; salted nuts will keep for 6–8 months, unsalted nuts 9–12 months.

For bottling or preserves

- Use good-quality, unblemished ripe fruit for jams and preserves.
- A crop of tomatoes that won't ripen will make excellent chutney, and recipes abound for things that you might not otherwise fancy eating but make great pickles or chutneys—marrows, chokos and the like.
- Don't forget marmalade when you are offered fruit from a neighbour's tree; juice can also be frozen for future use.
- Peaches and plums that won't ripen can still be bottled in syrup; the cooking process and the sugar will tenderise and sweeten what would otherwise be useless fruit.
- Slightly underripe fruits are easiest to peel and cook and will develop good colour and flavour once cooked. (Those peaches from the old tree that never fully ripen will be delicious when you eat them in a crumble during the winter.)

How to bottle using preserving jars

- Sterilise the jars you intend to use by placing them for at least 15 minutes in an oven heated to 120°C.
- Prepare seals by pouring boiling water over them and letting them become flexible. If reusing jam jars, boil the lids as if they were seals. The lids

must be modern ones with a plastic lining on the inside, not old metal ones. Discard any that have rust spots.
- I prefer a light syrup for preserving fruit, so the fruit flavours are not overpowered by the sugar. Combine the sugar and water in a large pan and bring to a gentle simmer. I use a ratio of 1 cup of sugar to 3 cups of water.
- To fill a standard large preserving jar you will need around 1kg of fruit.

Preparing fruit for bottling
- Apricots: wash, cut into halves and remove the stone.
- Peaches: peel and slice, or for small peaches leave them whole.
- Plums: wash, cut into halves and remove the stone, or leave whole.
- Pears: peel, cut into halves or quarters, and remove the core.

Cook the prepared fruit in the syrup until soft when pricked with the point of a knife. It should be just tender.

Using tongs, lift a hot clean jar out of the oven and place it in a heatproof dish. Pack the fruit into the hot jar (real preserving experts make an art of filling the jar in neat layers). When the jar is full to the rim, ladle in some very hot syrup then slip a long flexible knife (a filleting knife is ideal) down the insides of the jar to release air bubbles. Quickly top up the syrup and put on a seal so that when you press the seal down, excess syrup flows down the sides of the jar. Keeping pressure on top of the seal so no air gets in, screw the screw band into place.

Set the jar aside to cool. When it is completely cool, wash all the sticky syrup off the sides of the jar, add a label with the date, and store until required.

As the contents cool a vacuum is formed, and the seal will contract and become slightly concave. When you come to open the jar it will give a reassuring pop, confirming the contents are fresh.

Troubleshooting

Make sure every utensil is sterilised and that the jar, seal, fruit and syrup are scalding hot. If your seal does not form a vacuum when cool the filling was not hot enough. Remove the seal and reheat it in boiling water, place the full jar in the microwave and heat till the filling is boiling hot. Pour boiling water into the top of the jar until it overflows (yes, over the top of the existing fruit and syrup; you are just topping up and ensuring a good seal).

Replace the seal in the manner described above.

Chapter 4

IS YOUR HOME LEAKING MONEY?

You don't have to look hard to find places you can save money around the house. For the average household wanting to cut back, it's not so much about using less, it's about wasting less.

Of all our ongoing costs, the power bill is one of the heftiest 'fixed' household expenses, so it makes sense to try and trim it back first. We waste power every day. Though we can't actually see it leaking through the walls and trickling out of the lights, it is and we are paying for every single kilowatt—whatever a kilowatt is.

We'd save loads if we just used candles and huddled round them eating cold food out of cans and only bathed once a year, but I don't know anyone (apart from the odd teenage boy) who is prepared to live like that.

For me savings have got to be practical and not significantly diminish my quality of life, so I'm not suggesting you have to instigate two-minute showers and take to keeping your cup of tea water in the thermos so you only boil the jug once a day (although those teetering on the brink of financial disaster may want to consider such extreme measures).

Go through your house room by room and see if you are simply leaking money. The savings may be small initially, but a little bit each month makes a big difference over the course of a year.

Go through your house room by room and see if you are simply leaking money. The savings may be small initially, but a little bit each month makes a big difference over the course of a year.

While the power bill will always vary from month to month, it's still a 'fixed expense' because you have to pay it regardless. You may have thought you had little choice about the amount of power consumed and paid for in your house_ hold, but most of us can save some significant cash with small, consistent changes. It's also worth taking the time to check out the various deals offered by power providers in your area. There are some great online services that compare the power providers and then link you to the companies themselves for further information. For example, www.consumer.org.nz offers one called 'Powerswitch'.

How much power you use per day will vary from one household to another, but you may benefit from calculating an 'average' day's power expenditure for your household. Divide the total of your bill by the number of days in the billing period. This gives you a clear idea of what your comfort is costing you. How much could you save per year if you reduced your power bill by 20 per cent? What does a 'powerless day' save you?

You do need to have the household on board when it comes to power usage; there is little to gain if you are running around every day turning all the appliances off at the wall while your teenager or flatmate spends 45 minutes in the shower and leaves their electric blanket on all day.

Have a household meeting, discuss your expectations and explain why this is important.

> We have found it helps to have a goal. For example, 'If we can save X amount over the next three months, we'll be able to...' If that has no effect, then perhaps suggesting the removal of all non-essential electronic devices such as hair straighteners, phone chargers, PlayStations, cd players and TVs for a while might have the desired result.

Keeping the house warm is cheaper than warming it up

Heating consumes about one-third of your total power usage (35 per cent) and is one of the most significant costs whether you rent, flat or own your own home. **Insulation** reduces the amount of energy needed for heating or cooling your home.

- For every dollar spent on insulating old or cold houses, you get two dollars' worth of energy and health benefits.
- Nearly two-thirds of New Zealand's housing stock was built before insulation became mandatory in 1978. As a result, many of our houses don't have any insulation at all, or in some cases the insulation has been in place for years, and may no longer be doing its job properly.
- To minimise unnecessary expenditure on heating, first assess your insulation or lack of it.

No cost

- Maximise the free warmth of the sun by closing the curtains **before** it starts to get chilly.
- Close internal doors so you are only heating rooms that are in use.
- Check for draughts around window frames, french doors and under doorways. To locate the sources of draughts, close the curtains on a windy day and watch to see if they billow. If the curtains are flapping, you have a draught.
- Investigate draught-stopping options. The most immediate is simply to place a rolled towel along the bottom of the doorway, but there are effective specialised draught-stopping products for insulating around windows and doors. Even small improvements in insulation will pay for themselves, reducing your heating bill simply by keeping the warm air in and the cold air out.

- Simply switching appliances off at the wall instead of leaving them on standby can save you around $100 per year.

Low cost

- 25% of heat is lost through windows. Think about installing insulating window coverings if you live somewhere that gets cold. Thermally lined curtains are an easy, inexpensive and portable option for flatters and renters. Your thermal curtains will trap the heat in and shut the cold out.
- Rugs, carpet squares and mats will keep your feet from freezing; they also create a sense of cosiness and can be rolled away when not needed or shifted from one rental property to another.
- Lay a sheet of polythene on damp ground under the house to create a moisture barrier between the damp ground and your floorboards. You will have less mildew and the rooms will feel drier and warmer.

Long term

- Double glazing is worth considering for home owners in cold climates who are looking at long-term savings.
- Insulation for walls, floors and ceilings can make a huge difference to your power usage, as well as preventing damp and maintaining the value of your home.

- The effectiveness of insulation is measured by its 'R' value. The higher the R value, the more it slows down the transfer of heat. For example, an R3.0 product provides more insulation than an R1.0 product; with ceiling insulation, the R value gets higher as the product gets thicker. The R value you need depends on how cold it gets where you live. The Building Code specifies minimum R values, but it is a good idea to try to install more than the minimum where you can.
- Ripping out the walls and completely insulating an older house may not be financially viable, in which case installing under-floor or in-roof products is worth considering. They do a good job, and you don't want your expensive winter warmth drifting away through the floor and ceiling.
- Quality of installation is just as important as the quality of the insulation itself. Poor installation, creating gaps even as small as 2 mm, can reduce the performance of insulation by as much as 50%, so it's worth taking time to do it properly. Standards New Zealand have a comprehensive, easy-to-use guide on installing insulation (NZS4246:2006). You can download this free from www.energywise.govt.nz.
- Roof insulation can reduce heat loss by 35%, saving you $400 per year in colder areas. Underfloor insulation reduces heat loss by a further 14%, saving you even more.

- Under-floor insulation made from polystyrene products can be done in stages, starting with the most important or coldest rooms. You will gain the comfort of warm, dry rooms, and over time the investment will pay for itself.
- If you are considering buying or renting a property, check that it is insulated.
- If you live somewhere that was built before 1978 you may be eligible for subsidised insulation. Check out the EnergyWise website at www.enerygwise.org.nz for details. If you are a community services card holder and living in a rented property your landlord may be eligible.

Bathroom and laundry

Water heating accounts for roughly a third of your household energy consumption—all those long hot showers, dripping taps, or running the hot tap for ages while doing the dishes is simply pouring money down the drain.

No cost

- Check the temperature of your hot water; it should be set at 55–60°C. Any hotter is simply an expensive waste and in some cases can actually be dangerous. An extra 10°C could be costing you $140 per year.
- Turn the heated towel rails off when they're not needed. If everyone in your household showers

in the morning, use the heated towel rails to dry the towels during the day and turn them off overnight, or vice versa if you are a night-showering household. Using them for only a few hours a day instead of continuously can save you $100 per year. Turn them off completely over summer and dry the towels in the fresh air.

- Discuss the appropriate length of a shower. The flatmate (or teenager) who spends ages in the shower is costing you a lot of hard-earned money. A timer in the bathroom may seem draconian, but the people who take the longest showers will never believe that they do—or they'll insist that it takes that long for the shampoo and conditioner to do their thing.
- If you want to simply soak in hot water, have a bath and enjoy it. A quick shower uses less water than a quick bath, but a long shower will use more water than a long bath.

FYI

When we've used coin-operated showers in camping grounds that turn icy cold when your money runs out or leave you coated in soap because the water simply shuts off, the conditioner always manages to work much more quickly than it does at home.

- Wash laundry in cold water. Laundry-washing technology has improved to the degree that excellent results are possible with cold water in most cases. There is also less likelihood of colour loss and shrinkage, so your garments will last longer too.
- Don't use a clothes dryer unless you absolutely have to. Drying laundry outside saves power and makes it smell and feel better.

Low cost

- Reduce heat loss by wrapping your hot water cylinder in an insulated wrapper; if your electric storage cylinder and/or pipes feel warm to touch they are losing heat. Insulating the cylinder and the first metre of the hot pipe from the cylinder will help you get more value from the system; even wrapping an A-grade cylinder can deliver savings. There are a variety of wraps available from hardware stores, costing between $60 and $100. Installation instructions are on the packet.
- Install a low-flow shower head. The standard shower head with mains pressure delivers at least 12 litres of water a minute and often much more. Low-flow shower heads have flow restrictors built into the shower head. They reduce flow to about 7 litres a minute, saving water and energy—the overall cost savings can be considerable.

- To check your shower flow, run the shower at normal temperature. If it fills a 2-litre container in less than 12 seconds, it is running at a high flow rate and you could save a lot of money by using a more efficient shower head. These are available from hardware and plumbing stores.
- Low-flow shower heads give a good shower, using around half the water of a normal shower head. They cost roughly $40–$100, and can cut hot water bills by as much as $1000 per year! (Based on a family using the shower for 40 minutes a day, where the shower can fill a 2-litre container in 6 seconds.)
- Some shower heads will work just as well at low- and high-flow rates. If you have one of these that is currently running at a high-flow rate, you may be able to install a flow-restrictor disc. This goes between the pipe in the wall and the shower head.

Long term

- If you're building or renovating, consider putting a pressure reduction valve on the mains to reduce the water flow to the whole house. Discuss these options with your plumber.
- If purchasing a washing machine look for one with an Energy Efficient rating and an eco cycle, and one that will work efficiently using a cheap basic washing powder. Front loaders use very little water but may not clean as quickly as a top loader; work out what you need and do your research.

Types of heaters

Wood burners

Wood or pellet burners are the cheapest form of heating provided you have access to a supply of dry, untreated wood. I watched an undercover survey of firewood suppliers that screened recently on one of those TV consumer-watchdog-type shows. It revealed that the majority of firewood suppliers promoted their wood as dry when in actual fact most of it was too wet to burn effectively. The quantities supplied were generally accurate, the wood all came cut to the advertised size, it just needed to be stored longer before burning.

The simplest way to avoid buying wet wood seems to be to order your wood in the spring for the following winter so it has the whole summer to dry out. If you have an effective wood burner or range, adding in a wetback will supplement your hot water system, making it an energy-efficient and cost-effective heating system.

A wetback is a pipe arrangement that fits in the back of the firebox and uses heat from the fire to heat water. If you add a wetback, you'll get less heat in the room than you would without it, but if like ours the burner pumps out more heat than you actually need that is no great loss in exchange for the water heating gain.

The type and location of your hot water cylinder may well determine if you can fit a wetback or not; you'll need to check with both the fire manufacturer and a plumber.

Open fires

Open fires are significantly less effective than wood burners as most of the heat goes up the chimney, and they produce a lot of pollution. But an open fire gives a sense of welcome and cosiness that is very comforting. I love them.

Heat transfer systems

These make use of the heat generated by wood burners, using a fan to circulate the heat to other parts of the house.

Gas heating

Gas heating can be inexpensive on a per heat unit basis, but a properly ducted system may be costly to install. If you have access to natural gas then you could consider it as a long-term proposition.

Electric heaters

Electric heaters are cheap to purchase and provide effective heating, but the cost per heat unit is relatively high, particularly with radiant heaters. A cheaper option is an electric storage heater, such as an oil-filled heater which retains the internal heat once the oil has heated up, and will continue to generate warmth. They are pretty safe, portable and come in a variety of sizes. Use the right size for the room.

Gas/LPG heaters

These push out a decent amount of heat, but the benefits may be negated by the need to have a window open to allow fresh air to circulate, avoiding serious risks to your health.

Solar heating

Solar heating is expensive to install, even with subsidies, but as a long-term investment it makes sense. If you are building, factor it in.

Keeping warm

- It may seem obvious, but dressing appropriately for the weather can save you a lot in heating costs. Buy yourself a good-quality thermal undergarment and you won't need to hover over the heater all day. Wear slippers or socks and shoes if you are around the house in cold weather.
- Use winter-weight bedding during cold months.
- You may want to rearrange the furniture for cooler months, moving the seating away from windows where there is maximum heat loss and draught and arranging it nearer the fire or other heat

source. You'll be more comfortable and you won't be heating space you aren't using.

- Hot water bottles are cheap, safe and very effective for warming freezing feet on a cold night. If you are a frosty-footed one in winter the 'hottie' is much better than the electric blanket for heating feet.

Lighting

- Lights that are on most of the time add significantly to your power bill. A 150-watt security light left on all night (12 hours) will cost $90 a year. Replace it with a motion sensor security light, so it only switches on when it's needed.
- Downlights chew through even more electricity. A modern open-plan living/dining area could easily have 12 ceiling-mounted downlights. That's the equivalent of a one-bar heater in the ceiling. Replace the downlights with compact fluorescent bulbs (around $6 each) and consumption will be down to 240 watts. And, if the lights burn for six hours per night on average, this will save you $262 annually.

The consumer website www.consumer.org.nz has a comprehensive table of appliance running costs; you can use it to work out how to make the most effective savings in your home.

We bought both our kids electric blankets for the winter some years ago. My daughter loves hers but our boy, like me, prefers the hottie, because you can get the heat right where you need it (I've been known to have two all to myself). When I'm sitting at the computer all day, using the heater can make the room 'fuggy' without really making me feel warm. I find a hottie on my knees on those days works really well too.

Chapter 5

ROOM TO RENT

Sharing your home may not be your dream lifestyle, but an empty bedroom is a missed earning opportunity. Renting out your spare room will bring in a regular weekly income. If you don't have a spare bedroom, you may want to consider investing in a set of bunk beds and having your kids share a room for a while.

For a short-term cashflow top-up, a home-stay student or boarder may be the answer to your problems—a few weeks or a few months with an extra few bucks in the kitty may be all you need to get back on top or reach a savings goal.

Longer term you might want to consider a flatmate.

Either way, if you want to make some money without leaving home, and you have a spare bedroom, you could generate up to $10,000 per year by renting it out. You may have to spend a little up-front to advertise, furnish the room and make other adjustments, but having someone else in your home can be a life-enriching experience for all concerned. We've had experience with all the options outlined below and have also canvassed other experienced home-sharers for some of their tips. Everyone agreed that as a means to an end, renting out the spare room yields a good return for your investment.

For a short-term cashflow top-up, a home-stay student or boarder may be the answer to your problems—a few weeks or a few months with an extra few bucks in the kitty may be all you need to get back on top or reach a savings goal.

Low cost

Home-stay students

We have hosted A LOT of home-stay students over the years, and there are definitely pros and cons to the home-stay arrangement.

Home stay is essentially boarding, but the term is usually applied to visitors from overseas who pay to stay within the safety and security of a local household while they study.

Home-stay students usually prefer placement within a family or with a couple rather than in a single-person household, as the primary purpose of home stay is an authentic overseas experience. The opportunity for lots of English conversation and the chance to participate in 'family life' is usually of high importance.

Home-stay arrangements can be as short as a few days, or they may roll over from one year to the next. In most cases students will be enrolled in some type of schooling during the day, and older students may even have a part-time job if they are here for a while.

If the students are enrolled in a language school they may continue to attend classes even during our school holidays. This can be advantageous if you want to have some family time together without a guest in attendance. Students enrolled in local schools take school holidays like all the other pupils.

There are agencies that specialise in placing home-stay students, and they employ a specialist 'home-stay coordinator' to liaise with students, schools and host families. You may also see advertisements in the local paper for 'home-stay hosts' placed by local colleges. Students attending a local school will need 'local' accommodation.

Before you have a student it is likely you will receive a 'home inspection'. The student's room will need to have a bed, storage and a desk and chair. You will also be asked to provide references and undergo a police check.

Some schools and agencies arrange home stays for quite young children who are attending primary school. You can expect to be paid more for the additional responsibility of caring for a child. These children will depend on you for everything, may be homesick and tearful, reluctant to eat strange foods and very vulnerable (although they quickly adjust). Others will love the freedom of western childhood and education and will be a delight.

If you need time to yourselves as a household, then an older student may be a better option because they are more likely to develop their own social life. In many cases they may take off for whole weekends of sightseeing, or go out in the evenings with other friends.

Pros

- Support is available to home-stay hosts through the language school or home-stay coordinator if difficulties arise.
- You can host a short-term home-stay placement to 'dip your toes in' and see how your household copes with having someone else in the house. Knowing it's only for a fortnight will help you manage if it's not working out.
- There are standard rates for home-stay students, and payment is usually pretty secure, particularly if you use an agency.
- You get to learn about other cultures, which can be fun and interesting.
- Some cultures encourage politeness and helpfulness around the house (particularly with female students); this can be a real blessing.
- Students often feel more comfortable using their limited English to talk to children, so they'll chat and play with the kids when they get home in the evening, letting you get on with other stuff.
- You share in the students' excitement at new discoveries, and get to brag about your country, town and culture, all of which can be quite fun.

- Often schools organise both lessons and outings for the students, keeping them very busy, so you don't see much of them in the evenings as they have to study or are exhausted.
- A couple of home-stay students can make a big dent in the credit card bill or top up the holiday fund without too much extra 'work' on your part.
- Sometimes you can have two students at once (particularly if they are primary school age)—you can earn double the money and they'll keep each other company.
- You can specify the age, gender, even nationality of students you are prepared to take, and decline any that don't fit your brief.

While chatting with a Japanese student in our garden, I picked a ripe plum off the tree and gave it to her to eat. She bit into it then promptly burst into tears, explaining through her sobs that she had never in her life eaten anything 'just picked'. It was like an 'awakening' for her.

She was thrilled by the colour of the harbour—apparently Tokyo harbour was black—she'd never heard birdsong in the street before coming to New Zealand, and had rarely seen the stars. By the time she left us she'd swum with dolphins, walked up a mountain, been horse-riding, picnicked on the beach, spent hours gazing in wonder at the night sky and fallen in love with the great outdoors.

Cons

- Someone with limited English, away from home for the first time, needs emotional and practical support.
- Home-stay families must be willing to be 'family' to their student, helping with homework, transportation, communication, listening to problems, liaising with schools, and arranging things like doctors' appointments if needed—as well as just generally being willing to 'converse' with the student, explaining areas of culture and language even when they don't feel like it.
- If you are going on an outing or out to dinner you will probably have to take your student with you; they are part of your family for the duration of the arrangement. However, if you are going away or an emergency situation arises you may be able to arrange alternative accommodation for them through their home-stay coordinator.
- You may be expected to attend a 'graduation'-type ceremony at the end of the student's stay, and to drive them to an airport or pick-up point.
- Some students treat home-stay parents like staff. They can be lazy, rude, dishonest and sometimes worrying—most of them are teenagers, after all.

Home stays of three months or longer proved too much for us—we'd start to feel the need for our own space. Three weeks to a month was ideal. On the other hand, my friends Mary and Andy had many very successful long-term home stays (a year or longer) and had few complaints. You won't know till you try.

Our gorgeous Brazilian home-stay student was so much fun, we'll never forget her stay—she managed to join a football team, get mugged in a nightclub, hook up with a group of 20-something Arabian millionaires and find a part-time job all in her first week! She existed on a diet of chocolate and bananas, and was delighted with everything about New Zealand. She spoilt the kids rotten and we loved having her, even though we worried more about her than all the others put together!

The German fire-eater who snuck his girlfriends (plural) into his room and expected them to be served breakfast had to be 'relocated' by the agency.

Our Tahitian student stayed in bed studying with the heater on full tilt for the whole winter, emerging several times a day for long hot showers. But she was very sweet and easy to have around, although any financial advantage we may have gained from her stay was negated by the power bill!

Cultural differences can cause some tension in the home. One family I spoke to had a problem with a home-stay student who spoilt their little son while completely disregarding their slightly older daughter, and made no secret of the fact that it was because she was a girl. Others have told me of male home-stay students who treated women in the household with rude indifference, issuing orders, neglecting manners and making themselves pretty unpopular.

We have never had those problems ourselves, but it is important to make it clear where your family stands on certain areas and what is and is not culturally acceptable in your home.

We have had female students in particular who were very nervous around men and fascinated to see Kiwi dads playing with the kids, cooking, doing dishes or folding washing. One memorably plucked up the courage to ask 'What is Kiwi husband?' as it looked nothing like any model of 'husband' she had ever seen.

Loads of discussions about values, rights and cultural expectations followed (aided by the digital dictionary carried by most students).

Another sent me a card after her return home to let me know that she had broken up with the nasty boyfriend who, she had told me, had bullied her. She explained how she had gained confidence and self-respect living overseas, and I was glad I had taken the time to listen to her problems—like her mum.

Tips for first-time home-stay hosts

- From our own personal experience: the first two days are the hardest, while you help your student with public transport, alarm clocks, mealtimes, the need to keep you informed of their whereabouts, and explain about bathroom use (particularly important for Japanese students, who have different bathrooms and loos).
- It is likely that you will be presented with some small gifts and shown photos of the student's family and home town. If you have children this may mean you have to coach them to behave as if each time is the first time.
- Hosting short-term home stays involves a lot of 'first two days'; however, you also have the promise of having the house back to yourselves to look forward to at the end of each stint. All the home-stay host families I've talked to acknowledge that, regardless of the affection they may develop towards their students, and how many tears are shed on leaving day, all look forward to 'having the house back to themselves'.
- Longer-term home stays allow you to develop something of a routine and really get to know the student as their language and confidence develop. Great if you all get on; not so great if they are really winding you up, or taking advantage of your hospitality.
- Food is part of their 'cultural experience'. We always serve students the same meals as our family

is eating. I do know hosts who will try to cook specially to suit the tastes of their students. We don't do that—it's just not realistic, nor is it part of the deal. Plus it's fun to introduce them to our cuisine and spoil them with things that are commonplace to us but luxurious to them—ice cream, in particular. On the first day I do try to use ingredients that they will recognise, such as rice or noodles or beans.

- If students need a taste of home they can buy ingredients and prepare a meal from their culture to share with you—many take pride and pleasure in doing this. If you are in a city there are loads of ethnic places where they can buy lunch for a taste of home.
- It is not acceptable to feed the student different meals to the family to increase the profitability of the arrangement!

Boarders

Boarding is a popular and sensible option for students, people on short-term secondment to a new town or young people newly out of the nest.

It can also be attractive to oddballs who don't fit into a regular flatting situation, which means they probably won't fit into your home either!

If you are approached by mature adults seeking board for no obvious reason, ask a lot of questions. Find out about their employment—having a proper job where they work and interact with a variety of people and enjoy it is a good indicator of a socially well-adjusted individual. Moving from one boarding situation to another, working on their own, or from home (your home if you take them on) or only working part-time is often not a good sign. Consider their age and stage of life. What are most average 27-year-old men doing, and why is this one not doing the same as his peers? If you have young children it is not unreasonable to insist on doing a police check. If they were coming into your house as a cleaner they'd have been checked out by the police first—if they're going to be living in your house it's even more important. Better to be safe than sorry.

If they work from home, they are going to be around your house all day. Part-time workers will also be around more than someone working an eight-hour day. The part-time worker will also have less disposable income, making it less likely that they'll be out and about at the weekends. You may end up spending far more time with the boarder than you ever intended.

The other area where we've found some judicious questioning is worthwhile is on the topic of food. If the prospective boarder is female, over the age of 23 and a picky eater, in our experience the funny food issues may be disguising an eating disorder. Before you know it your boarder is leaving the table halfway through dinner to wash the sauce off the chicken casserole and bingeing out of your fridge in the middle of the night. Avoid, avoid, avoid!

> One family talked about the time their boarder decided to host a full-on blokey poker party the same day as their regular women's coffee group get-together. The poker party was in full swing as carloads of mums and toddlers were arriving upstairs for coffee and cake—talk about two different worlds colliding!

These people need professional help, not your kind listening ears. You can all too easily find yourself being drawn into the role of counsellor, making it even harder to give them the boot if they're driving you mad, defaulting on their payments or wearing you out with their 'needs'. Ask lots of questions, get references and be blunt if you have to. It's a financial arrangement first and foremost.

In a standard boarding situation the boarder will expect a furnished room—bed, lighting, storage and in many cases bedding and linen to be provided—as well as breakfast and dinner.

A boarder will pay more per week than a flatmate, but would not be expected to share in household responsibilities and decision-making, such as putting out the rubbish, doing the vacuuming or preparing meals. It is reasonable to expect a boarder to clean up after themselves, however, and keep their room clean.

Someone offering 'board' should not expect to have to cater for the boarder's friends or family, or overnight guests, unless this has been previously arranged with you and any additional expenses discussed.

> We had a boarder for three years with great success. If everyone gets on well and problems are sorted out speedily your boarder may become a life-long friend.
>
> We developed a routine so one night a week she had the house to herself; we'd put our kids to bed and go out (YIPPEE!), leaving her free to have friends around for coffee or just enjoy the sense of having her own place, while keeping an ear out for the kids. The routine suited all of us, gave us all space and was lots of fun.
>
> Fortunately for us she loved our kids, and we were able to support and encourage her through her studies when her own family were far away. Both my husband and I felt that it was like having a sister living with us. We enjoyed watching her romances unfold, and celebrated exam results with her.
>
> The boarding arrangement ended happily when she left on her wedding day to be married to my sister's boarder.

People newly out of relationships can find boarding a good short-term solution while they get their affairs sorted out and find a permanent new address. In some cases they may want to be able to have their kids stay overnight in their room and will pay extra for expenses accordingly.

Long term

Flatmates

Open any paper and you will see loads of ads for flatmates. Before shelling out cold hard cash on an ad of your own, and introducing a flatmate to your household, be realistic about what you are offering and what impact the flatmate will have on the household.

Professional sharers and student flats are quite different ends of the flatting experience spectrum and will attract different types of people.

If you have a stylish, comfortable, modern environment you will likely be able to charge more, expect a professional or fully employed person to apply, and they'll expect their home to be well maintained and worth the money.

If it's a run-down hovel with leaky pipes and stinky carpet, you are more likely to pick up a student. Their money is as good as anyone's, and will help you fix the leaky pipes and replace the carpet in the long term, but you won't be able to charge as much, and they may not be as concerned about keeping things clean and neat.

What are you offering?

- Does it matter to you if the flatmate is male or female?
- Is the room a single or double, is it furnished or unfurnished, with or without an en suite bathroom? How many bathrooms does the house have?
- Will you take smokers? Pets?
- Will you be operating on shared or separate food and expenses?
- Is there off-street parking? What is the proximity to amenities such as malls, parks and public transport?
- Are you after long or short term? Has the house got broadband? Views? All-day sun?

What they'll expect

- A flatmate will expect equal rights in your home, including inviting friends around, sharing in household decision-making and other household responsibilities. If you have kids, the flatmate will need to be family oriented, as the kids are likely to bond with them.
- The flatmate is also likely to be around during family events such as birthdays, Christmas and long weekends.
- The flatmate will also have extended family and may have kids—how do you feel about extra kids or girlfriends and boyfriends sleeping over?
- The flatmate will have friends of their own, who will visit—how will you handle the social aspects

of the arrangement? Do you have more than one lounge or living space? Can you fit a couple of old couches and a coffee table into the kitchen/dining area to provide a second 'lounge'? Will you allow coffee- and tea-making stuff in the bedroom?

People unused to sharing should perhaps consider boarders or home-stay students as opposed to flatmates, as the egalitarian nature of flatting may cause feelings of resentment or of the home having been usurped. Try out these scenarios:

- You've invited someone around for a visit and get home to find the flatmate has some friends around already...
- You go to put on a load of washing and find the machine already full of the flatmate's clothes...
- You walk in the door after a hard day, longing to collapse in front of your favourite show on TV, and find the flatmate in front of the telly, settled in and halfway into a DVD marathon...
- You find your flatmate is poking around in the kitchen in their dressing gown and slippers at 11 o'clock on a Saturday morning when you have people coming for lunch at 12...

If you are gritting your teeth already, it's possible that having a flatmate may not be the best option for you. But you might make a great 'home-stay host family'.

FYI

Friends of ours, a married couple, 'flatted' for a couple of years with a group of colleagues, one of whom had recently purchased the house. They enjoyed the stimulation of other company in the evening, the sharing of household tasks, and the chance to have a garden and pets. They also liked that they were helping their friend get on the property ladder.

The arrangement worked so well for them that when a job shift moved them away, they opted to flat with others again in their new neighbourhood.

All of these options will require some work on your part. It may be that the work is simply setting up the room and after that everything is easy, or it may be that preparing an extra meal and interacting with an extra person every day is hard work to you. If that is the case, make sure you are being appropriately remunerated for the work. As my mum used to say, 'You can cry all the way to the bank'.

Chapter 6

CLEAN UP YOUR ACT

I have to confess that I am not a 'cleanie'. When the dust bunnies escape from behind my fridge, I consider it's time to move.

Hygiene is important though. We want to stay healthy even if we can't manage tidy, so that means a regular cleaning regimen.

The average household has come to expect a standard of household hygiene unimaginable 100 years ago, spawning a multi-billion-dollar cleaning industry. There are now so many cleaning products and tools available it's tempting to buy a lot of pricey stuff we don't actually need.

So before running amok in the cleaning aisle of the supermarket, consider the fact that most of the 'essential' cleaners can be made inexpensively from things you probably already have to hand. Home-made cleaning products are easy to make and pretty effective, they're generally less irritating to sensitive skins, and you can even reuse your existing spray cleaner bottles to store them in.

Baking soda, white vinegar and bleach in various combinations will clean most surfaces hygienically, cheaply and with little impact on the environment.

For the serious stuff—ovens and the like—ammonia and borax may come into play.

Always label what's in the container with a permanent marker. Include all the ingredients. (It's not unheard of for small children to attempt to drink or ingest by various other means household cleaners. I personally can claim to having had a good go at the rat poison in my preschool years.) In this situation you will need to know the ingredients in order to get appropriate medical attention.

It's also a good idea to write the recipe for the mix right on the bottle with a permanent marker, for easier mixing the next time.

Baking soda, white vinegar and bleach in various combinations will clean most surfaces hygienically, cheaply and with little impact on the environment.

Kitchen

Dishes

- Dishwash-liquid extender will make the liquid last three times as long with no reduction in grease-cutting ability. It leaves dishes sparkling clean and hands soft. This mixture is very useful when the kids do the washing up, as they are inclined to use way more detergent than an adult doing the same job.

Make a dishwash-liquid extender from:

1Tbsp washing soda
1 1/2 cups very hot water
1 cup dishwashing detergent

Dissolve the washing soda in the water, and stir in the detergent. Decant into a container and shake before use.

Washing soda is a natural compound, and it is available in the cleaning section of some supermarkets or in hardware stores. It's really inexpensive, and also forms the basis of scented bath crystals.

Dishwasher powder

- Replace commercial dishwasher powder with a mixture made from equal quantities of borax and baking soda. Add fragrance such as lemon with a drop of essential oil.
- Washing soda also works well in the dishwasher in place of dishwasher powder, but we find the glassware becomes cloudy after a while; sparkling glassware depends on using a rinse aid. White vinegar works as a satisfactory rinse aid.

Dishwasher

- To clean a gungy dishwasher (oh dear, maybe it's only my dishwasher that gets yucky inside?), fill both detergent containers with baking soda and run it through a complete cycle. The dishwasher will be clean and odour-free.

Microwave

- The inside of my microwave frequently resembles an artwork by Jackson Pollock. To remove the spatters and squiggles of previous meals easily, dissolve a couple of tablespoons of baking soda in water in a microwave-safe bowl, then bring to the boil in your microwave. Let it sit for a minute or two, then you should easily be able to wipe out any baked-on stains; the microwave will smell fresh too (again, is it only me who has to do this?).

Oven

Rich decided to clean the oven for me a while back. It took three days and he had to use a paint scraper. It was marvellous afterwards, of course. The kids were fascinated to discover that the square glass bit in the middle of the door was actually a window and kept dashing back into the kitchen to watch the pastry rising. But after a week or two the glass got murky, and the prospect of doing it all again made us lose the will to live. The best way to manage oven cleaning is to get it clean, then keep it clean.

- For light cleaning, sprinkle with baking soda and mist with water. Leave for several hours, or overnight, then wipe clean. You will have no nasty oven-cleaner smell or taste to contend with afterwards, and no horrid chemicals. A green scouring scrubber pad can be useful for the hard speckly bits on racks and the window.

- For a heavily soiled oven (mine) you'll need to break out the strong stuff. Ammonia is a very inexpensive cleaning agent, but it can be toxic, so use with care. **Do not ever mix ammonia with bleach as it creates an extremely toxic gas, and use ammonia only in well-ventilated areas.** Place a cup of ammonia in the oven and leave it with the door closed overnight. The ammonia will loosen grime from the surfaces. Ventilate the kitchen before opening the oven, and use rubber gloves when you wipe out the residue. If you need to, scrub with baking soda and water and a green scouring pad. Rinse with warm soapy water to remove any ammonia residue.

Sinks

- Sprinkle the sink with baking soda and wipe with a damp sponge. This works just as well as a cream or paste cleaner on porcelain or stainless steel. (I have a white porcelain sink in the kitchen and a stainless steel one in the scullery, and I use it on both.) You can make a paste of baking soda and water for spreading with a sponge, or you can put the baking soda in a shaker (a plastic icing-sugar shaker works well).

Taps

- Spread a thin paste of baking soda on taps, and when dry polish off with a rag for the shiniest, shiniest taps you've ever seen.

Fridge

- Dissolve a couple of tablespoons of baking soda in a bowl of warm water and wipe the interior for a clean and odour-free fridge.
- Keep a small dish of baking soda uncovered in the fridge to absorb odours. Replace it every month, and use the old baking soda to clean the drain. Pour it in and wash down with a couple of cups of boiling water.

Laundry

The old-fashioned idea of wearing smocks, aprons and pinnies so you only had to spot-clean your clothes saved a whole lot of laundry. But until it becomes a fashion trend on MTV I'm resigned to 'moundles' of teenage laundry. (The word 'moundle' was coined by a friend's preschooler—it aptly described the towering pile of washing created by the preschooler and her twin. Feel free to apply it to your own washing heap.)

Washing wears clothes out quickly and causes colours to fade. Try not to wash simply because something has been worn once. Is it actually dirty, does it smell? If there is no visible dirt or detectable odour it doesn't need washing. Kids, I've noticed, are inclined to pile stuff in the laundry basket because it's easier than hanging clothes up or putting them away. Try and convince them to sort the clothing and only wash what is needed.

Follow the washing instructions on clothes. I avoid buying 'dryclean only' clothing as it's expensive to dryclean. Many garments now come with dryclean labels simply because the manufacturers want to protect themselves against complaints if the garment shrinks or fades. It's a real pain. Generally, cotton, linen, rayon, silk and polyester-based garments can be safely laundered at home.

Woollens

- Woollen garments are best washed on a gentle or woollen cycle, or handwashed in warm, soapy water. Don't spin your woollens dry in the washing machine either, as this causes the fibres to matt together and the garment may become stretched from the weight of the waterlogged wool as it spins. Squeeze excess moisture out by hand—do not wring. Lay the garment on a folded towel and roll it up, then press on the towel to blot the water out of the wool.
- Lie the garment flat on a dry towel, arranging it carefully so it retains its shape. Dry out of direct sunlight.

Stains

- Make a paste from baking soda and water and rub it into the stain prior to washing.

Washing powder

- Washing powder isn't hugely expensive, but nor is it particularly kind to the environment. This easy home-made powder works well. Finely grate 1 bar of soap (use a processor if you have one, or get the kids to do it while they watch a movie). Combine the grated soap with 1/2 cup washing soda and 1/2 cup borax. Use around 1Tbsp per load.

Borax

- Commonly used as a laundry booster, borax makes washing come out cleaner, minus stains and odours that normal laundry detergents leave behind. All you need to do is add a 1/2 cup to your washing machine at the beginning of the wash cycle.
- Alternatively, add a tablespoon of baking soda to a wash with regular laundry detergent. It will soften, remove soap residue and brighten colours.

Bathroom

- Make up a bulk batch of all-purpose surface cleaner. In a well-ventilated area, combine 50ml white vinegar, 50ml cloudy ammonia and 1/2 cup baking soda in 4 litres of hot water. Using rubber gloves, pour the liquid into an empty storage bottle and fill pump-action spray bottles. Use the mix either on a damp cloth or as a spray and wipe to clean benches, baths, showers, etc. Shake well before use.

- For a smaller amount of all-purpose cleaner fill a spray bottle with equal quantities of white vinegar and water. Any vinegar smell will disappear once surfaces have dried. Vinegar is a natural deodoriser. This mixture is effective for dissolving soap scum and cleaning most surfaces. I wouldn't use it on marble or granite.
- Remove soap scum by making a paste from vinegar and baking soda and applying it to murky shower screens. Works as well as any commercial product I've tried.
- Instead of buying those expensive 'spray and walk away' shower cleaners, use one of the above regularly.

The loo

- All-purpose spray cleaner, baking soda, bleach or white vinegar will all clean the loo hygienically and cheaply.

Windows and mirrors

- Vinegar in water, or just good old warm water, crumpled newspaper and elbow grease, will clean windows pretty well, or you can fill a sprayer bottle with 1 cup rubbing (isopropyl) alcohol, 1 cup water and 1Tbsp white vinegar. Or just shut the curtains.

Follow a routine

Are you clueless as to what to clean when? In the olden days, every day had its set tasks: Monday was baking day, Tuesday was washing day ... Those simple routines ensured that all the necessary tasks were completed, and everyone followed a similar routine.

Having some sort of a schedule will help you keep on top of tedious tasks so they don't mount up. Keeping a house clean is important for good health and to take care of your assets. If you do a little each day the main stuff is covered by the end of the week. Some things only need doing fortnightly or monthly, so if you alternate those tasks and hit a few each week as you do the daily stuff you'll have a clean house, you won't need to fork out money on lots of specialist products, things like curtains and carpets will stay looking good longer and they'll be free of mildew because your windows and sills are regularly cleaned.

FYI

Baking soda

Baking soda alone has loads of uses around the house; here are just a few:

• **Natural deodorant** Sprinkle or pat pure baking soda on your armpits for a natural deodorant.

• **Smelly shoes** Sprinkle a generous amount into smelly shoes to reduce odours.

• **Toothpaste** Make a thick paste, apply to your toothbrush and use as you would any other toothpaste. You can add peppermint essence to disguise the nasty flavour.

• **Antacid** Use about a teaspoon in a small glass of water and drink, to reduce the effects of an acid stomach.

• **Bites and stings** Mix a thick paste of baking soda and water and apply to the bites to reduce itching, swelling and the pain from stings.

• **Freshen carpets** Sprinkle with baking soda then vacuum up.

• **Deodorise kitty litter** Sprinkle the litter tray with baking soda.

Daily

- **Bedrooms:** make beds, open curtains and open a window to allow some fresh air to circulate.
- **Kitchen:** Put away all dishes, wipe the sink and clean the stove and all benchtops. Replace dish towels and hand towels.
- **Laundry:** Depending on the size of your household, you may need to put on a load of laundry before bed at night so it's ready to hang out in the

morning before work or the other busyness of the day takes over.

Weekly

- Clean bathrooms, including toilets, bath, basins and mirrors; restock toilet rolls.
- Wash bathroom, kitchen, laundry floors.
- Replace sheets and towels with clean ones.
- Vacuum all regularly used rooms such as bedrooms, living areas, dining room or office. Guest rooms can be done less frequently.
- Wipe out one pantry shelf each week, discarding any damaged or dated foods.
- Iron clothing as needed. Fold and put away clean laundry in correct cupboards and drawers.

Fortnightly

- Dust all surfaces.
- Wipe kitchen cupboard fronts and appliances, and clean microwave and bins. Wipe out fridge.
- Clean shower stalls.

Monthly

- Wipe handles, light switches and door knobs; wipe window sills.
- Dust high places for cobwebs. For cleaning up high or under, put an old sock over the end of a stick or broom handle and secure with a rubber band. Slide under the fridge, behind the shelves

and up into difficult corners to remove dust and cobwebs easily.

- Replace any spent light bulbs.

Three-monthly

- Clean behind and under large items of furniture.
- Clean the oven if needed.
- Clean windows.
- Have a good chucking-out session of accumulated junk and sort out any outstanding paperwork, throwing out any out-of-date papers, magazines etc. (or become one of those people who have to climb over their junk collections to get to their beds).
- Check the flea and worming schedules for the pets.

Real dyed-in-the-wool cleanies might like to create a schedule so everyone knows which week you are up to: last week we washed all the cupboard fronts and wiped out the fridge, this week we need to do the shower stalls and clean the bins and microwave. Next week is the first week of the month, that's when we give all the knobs and switches a quick clean.

You don't have to do it all at once. A spring-clean can give you a good feeling for a day or two, but a few minutes each day will keep everything clean and sparkling and ensure that the less-frequent jobs don't get forgotten until next spring.

How to reduce ironing

My mother-in-law likes to iron, she even irons knickers and socks. Admittedly, ironing can be therapeutic if you've nothing better to do. Personally, I'd rather go to the dentist than spend an hour ironing, so I use these tips to keep the ironing to an absolute minimum.

- Overloading the washer or dryer will increase the likelihood of clothing wrinkling. Make sure that each load you put in has plenty of room for tumbling.
- Try not to overdry garments or sheets, as too much heat can set wrinkles.
- A fabric softener will help your garments stay soft during drying or airing.
- Try not to dry washing in the baking sun as this results in crisp, stiff clothes that are hard to iron.
- Hang shirts upside down by the side seams to avoid the imprint of peg marks being visible.
- Using the correct iron temperature is also very important. Make sure you read the garment care instructions on your piece of clothing. As a general rule cotton and linen are easier to iron when slightly damp.

Cleaning as a way to earn money

Cleaning is a great way to earn a little extra cash. A good hardworking cleaner can earn more than a nurse, office administrator, home carer or retail assistant. Hourly rates vary, but with good references and the willingness to work up a sweat, cleaning is a good earner.

- You can register with an agency, who will interview you, check references, do a police check, etc. and try and find you a placement. They may also take a cut from your pay.
- You can advertise yourself—local papers and letter-box drops may be the best way to find work in your neighbourhood. Is your neighbourhood likely to be a lucrative source of cleaning work or do you need to go further afield?
- Be clear about what you will and won't do—cleaning ovens, for example, or ironing. Some cleaners won't do windows or anything above arms' reach.
- Some cleaners will tidy as they go, others just clean. Your clients will need to know exactly what they are getting for their money.
- You will need to determine who supplies what—do you bring all your own equipment and products or use theirs? If you are supplying your own you must be sure they are safe to use on the surfaces in the clients' property.
- A domestic cleaner needs to employ exemplary hygiene practices, using separate cloths and gloves for loos and sinks, removing shoes before stepping into showers, etc.

Cleaning is physical work, and it's tiring. You need to have a reasonable degree of fitness to seriously consider cleaning as an income stream. You can expect to be lugging vacuum cleaners up and down stairs, bending over baths, scrubbing in corners and dusting above your head. The advantages are that the hours are often quite flexible, so the work can be fitted in around school hours or uni lectures; it requires little in the way of experience or set-up; rates are competitive, and you can get yourself up and running quickly.

Prospective clients will expect to be offered character references and may want to have a police check done—this is perfectly fair and reasonable when they are allowing a stranger into their home. So you need to have copies of references available, and phone numbers of people who are willing to give you a verbal reference.

> It's easy to become slapdash over time. A good way to keep yourself motivated is to imagine there is a hidden camera operating and you could find yourself appearing on a national TV show about worst workers caught on camera—you may have seen the type of thing, where the plumber is caught going through the client's knicker drawer, or the cleaner swigs out of the liquor cabinet and wipes the baby's highchair with the corner of a filthy T-shirt...

Chapter 7

WHEN THE RUBBER HITS THE ROAD

As a family, we've clocked up thousands of kilometres touring in our tired old station wagon. In our early years we were simply enjoying family camping holidays. In recent years the travelling has been a necessary part of presenting destitute gourmet cooking demonstrations around the country in big cities, small towns and everything in between. We've done some nightmare drives, travelling from Auckland to Dunedin in two and a half days in a car laden with pumpkins and trays of eggs, with our two small children tucked into their car-seats dozing and playing endless games of 'I spy with my little eye...'

We've sneaked through the Lewis Pass minutes before snow closed the road, we've crossed the Crown Range, driven the Forgotten Highway in filthy weather and traversed the Takaka hills, there and back on the wettest, foggiest day in history. We've frequently spent five or six weeks at a stretch travelling with our modest car loaded to the gunnels (whatever they are) and the kids wedged in the back seat. We've toured with toddlers and we've toured with teens.

We travelled by car because it was cheaper than flying, enabled us to be together as a family, and we could carry all the necessary gear for the demonstrations that were booked. We've seen a lot more of the countryside than most over the years; consequently, we think we know a thing or two about car journeys.

Tips for travelling on the cheap

Car travel is an affordable way to get from A to B, and it can be enjoyable and even memorable. Part of the success of a trip lies in your mindset; you have to appreciate the journey itself and not just focus on the destination. But the vast majority of journeys people take are not long ones—whether it's the daily drive to the office or the annual holiday, thinking about the way you drive and planning your travel can save you a lot of cash.

Your driving style and how well or poorly you maintain your vehicle will impact on how much you spend on fuel. A well-maintained older vehicle can be a more cost-effective proposition than shelling out on upgrading to a newer car.

A well-maintained older vehicle can be a more cost-effective proposition than shelling out on upgrading to a newer car.

You can make significant reductions in fuel consumption by adopting the following fuel-efficiency driving tips, developed by the Energy Efficiency and

Conservation Authority (EECA). For further information visit their website at www.eeca.govt.nz.

- Avoid unnecessary travel by car. One-third of car trips in New Zealand are less than 2 km, and two-thirds are less than 6 km. For some trips you could use public transport, walk or cycle; car pool (e.g. group together to deliver and pick up children, go to and from work); plan trips to reduce the distance and number you take by car (this will also reduce cold engine running, which can increase fuel consumption by up to 40% over a short trip).
- Drive with a smile. Less aggressive driving practices can improve fuel economy by up to 30%.
- You could: go easy on the pedal; accelerate smoothly through the gears—change early but do not labour the engine; look ahead—maintain appropriate distances to avoid heavy breaking and acceleration.
- Keep within the speed limit and what is safe for the road conditions; driving at 90kph instead of 110kph saves 25% of fuel consumption.
- Avoid congestion—plan your trip and timing to save both fuel and aggravation.
- Ease off the accelerator when approaching the top of a hill—you will naturally pick up speed as you crest the hill.
- Maintain your vehicle. Better car maintenance can add up to a 10–20% improvement in fuel consumption.

- Keep tyres inflated to the manufacturer's recommended pressure—7 psi too low results in a 2–3% increase in fuel consumption. Remember to check the tyres when they are cold; make sure wheel alignments are checked regularly.
- Make sure that engine timing, air filter and spark plugs are checked regularly.
- Keep vehicle load to a minimum. Removing roof racks and roof-rack loads when they are not required can result in a possible 5–10% improvement in fuel economy. Remove unnecessary weight, as an additional 50-kg load increases fuel consumption by 2%. But remember, it's good for overall fuel economy to fill up the car with people going to a common destination.
- Closing windows and sunroofs when travelling at open-road speeds can result in up to 5–7% improvement in fuel economy.
- Reduce the use of accessories. The air conditioner could add 10% to fuel consumption. Use air vents rather than air conditioning when you can, and use the rear screen demister only when needed as it could increase fuel consumption by 3–5%.

Engine tips

- Switch off the engine if idling for more than 30 seconds, and always allow plenty of time to restart your engine. Also, when starting from cold, stay light on the throttle for the first few minutes.

- Longer term: choose the right vehicle for your needs; for example, large 4WDs make expensive commuter vehicles. Try to find out the fuel economy of the vehicle you are thinking of buying; in general, the smaller the engine capacity the better the fuel consumption.

Plan ahead

Even without the luxury of first-class comfort and five-star hotels at every stop you can stay healthy, active and in budget throughout your journey if you plan ahead. Whether you are driving for work or pleasure, on your own or with the family, you might find some of my top-10 travelling tips helpful for surviving the rigours of the road trip.

1. **Hydration:** sipping cold water frequently keeps everyone awake and alert. Write each person's name on their water bottle in permanent marker. Chill water bottles overnight at each stop. Avoid sugary drinks and juice while travelling, as they are more likely to cause sickly feelings on winding roads, they make everything sticky if they get spilt, and are no good whatsoever for topping up the radiator, rinsing off sand or mopping up after a blood nose—the water bottle has more uses than just drinking.
2. **Toilets:** loo stops are a good opportunity for everyone to stretch their legs. Big flash gas stations and fast-food outlets generally have reasonable toilet facilities and air conditioning,

but also lots of temptations in the form of junk food and lollies which are bad news on long trips. Think sticky, queasy and costly. Use the public facilities when you can; they're usually well-sign-posted and well-maintained even in small towns. Parking further up the street gives you more of a wake-up walk too, which is really important on long journeys. You don't want the driver getting the drowsies. Keep some 'hand sanitiser' and a box of tissues in the glove box in case the facilities aren't great—you'll also be OK if the worst comes to the worst and you have to make an emergency stop in the wild.

3. **Snacks:** car snacking is inevitable. I find I snack when I'm travelling on my own as it's hard to drift off to dreamland when you are crunching through something. Snacks keep the energy levels up and break the monotony of a long, featureless drive. As a savoury snack we favour popcorn—it is messy but it's healthy and cheap and keeps the kids busy for a long time. We also take chewing gum, rice crackers, grapes, little bags of baby carrots and some apples, and we'll buy an occasional Popsicle although we avoid ice cream on long journeys—creamy stuff isn't good for windy roads and stuffy cars. The same goes for chippies and lollies—too sticky and queasy-making.
4. **Meal breaks:** try small, frequent snacks rather than scoffing a big lunch then jumping into the

car and embarking on hours of driving. A big meal can make you feel sleepy, or sickly if the roads are bad. We've found that a good solution is to prepare small filled rolls, each wrapped individually as not everyone will necessarily feel hungry at the same time. The rolls can be dished out as needed and the small packages are easy to manage and quick to prepare. If you do end up having to purchase food en route, avoid the gas station 'café', where you'll pay a premium for mediocre sandwiches or greasies from the hot cabinet. Stretch your legs with a quick dash around the local grocery store or supermarket—a pot of yoghurt, some fruit or fresh rolls and deli meat makes an inexpensive and healthy meal on the run. Many supermarkets now sell ready-made sandwiches that are fresh and tasty and much less expensive than those from a gas station or café. The bakery departments also frequently sell savoury breads, scones and muffins, which are filling, and while more expensive than a home-made option, are much cheaper than café versions.

5. **Cafés:** eating out on the road is a bit of a lottery. You might get lucky and find a gem of a café or restaurant. If the choices are limited and you really need a hot meal, in our experience the safest option is generally the 'all-day breakfast'. It's pretty hard to ruin bacon, eggs and toast, and even if it isn't great, it's usually edible. Because

it all has to be cooked fresh for each order it's a safer option than something that gets reheated in the microwave and may have been hanging around for a while. Only buy sandwiches from refrigerated cabinets. They should be individually wrapped, and if they don't feel cool to the touch avoid, avoid, avoid. I've picked up sandwiches that have been sitting in a non-refrigerated cabinet all day and that felt positively warm to the touch. On further investigation they had been made 18 hours earlier and not refrigerated at all. I'd rather go hungry than go to hospital in a strange town. When you order a hot meal it should arrive 'piping hot'. If it's not hot all the way through, or is only warm, send it back! You can do without food poisoning while you are travelling (speaking from experience). Refrigeration inhibits but does not prevent the development of food-borne bacteria, nor will it kill any bacteria already present. Thorough heating is the only way to be sure reheated food is safe to eat. I always treat chicken, ham, seafood and boiled eggs with caution. Evening meals can be a big expense when you are travelling, and even if you have cooking facilities in your accommodation they are likely to be basic. If you are planning to cook in a motel, keep it simple, as the presence of even very basic equipment such as a sieve or a sharp knife can't be assumed. When you are required to eat out, you have only to be away for a few days before you realise that there is only one kids' menu in the whole country, and every single restaurant is offering it—kids' burger and chips, chicken nuggets and chips, or fish bites and chips with ice cream for dessert. The kids' menu offers fried food and not much else.

FYI

We have rarely ever found a kids' menu offering a proper meal which has not been fried. We longed to see even something simple that would appeal to the kids but wasn't fried, like sausages and mash or little cottage pies, or kids' roast chicken and veges, but it was always the same—fried, fried, fried.

The kids love it, of course. We learned to intercept the menu before it was presented to them, to forestall the inevitable pleading. Much as they might like it, we won't let our kids order fried food more than once a week, and when you are travelling it's hard to avoid.

We've had to explain over and over again to restaurant staff that we can't use the kids' menu because it's exactly the same as the last three nights and the kids need to eat real food. In some cases they've allowed us to pick through the main menu, ordering the spuds off one dish and the chicken and veg from another and then plating it into two smaller portions—not everywhere is as obliging! But if you can find a staff member who looks likely to be a parent you are in with a chance.

6. **The cheapest and best-value option for family dining** we've found is the weekend roast. Lots of pubs, clubs and restaurants do a roast dinner at a set price, which may include a dessert and drink too. Small towns may have a 'club' that serves meals, and some B and B's will also provide an evening meal on request. This may prove more cost-effective and less stressful than eating out. Motels that cater to regular commercial travellers may offer home-cooked meals in the rooms—this is also likely to be a cheaper option than eating out. Stock up on fresh fruit, and take your own breakfast foods. We keep a chilly bin in the boot, with bread, spreads, milk, etc. Even if you are only away for a day or two, a good breakfast before you leave each morning is important and you'll save heaps by taking your own.
7. **Be vigilant with hand hygiene:** when you are travelling you come into contact with surfaces that hundreds of people may have touched before you—from toilet door handles and playground equipment to café chairs and counter tops. Use wet wipes or hand sanitiser when you return to your car. If that seems a little OCD, it's worth remembering that you are likely to be eating with those germy fingers later when you are in the

car, miles from anywhere, without a sink and bar of soap handy for washing your hands. Also, the exterior of the car gets really dirty. If you have to open the dusty boot, check the oil or deal with a dirty nappy you'll want to clean your hands afterwards.

8. **Amusements:** on long journeys boredom is inevitable at some point. Stock up on free talking books before you leave; they're available from your local library. When our kids were little we'd all listen to story tapes and songs, then eventually the kids would drop off and we'd drive as far as we possibly could before they woke up, knowing that once they woke we'd probably need to stop, have a drink, maybe find a playground or stretch the legs a bit. Some people drive at night so the kids can sleep and not moan about being bored. This never worked for us as it didn't suit our schedule, and night driving has its own challenges. We've listened to all the Narnia books, all the Harry Potters, lots of Malory Blackman and Jacqueline Wilson. We found that listening to the stories whet the children's appetites to read the books again for themselves, and made the time pass easily, and we enjoyed hearing them too. The kids aren't the only ones who enjoy having something to listen to. There are loads of talking book options for adults. Most recently we listened to Terry Waite's autobiography *Taken on Trust,* read by the man himself. However, if you are

planning to play adult talking books in the car you may want to consider the suitability of the material for younger listeners so that you don't find yourself suddenly lurching for the off button!

As our kids got older they had their own portable CD players which have been invaluable on long journeys. They can each listen to their own selection, and they can use dual headphones if they both want to listen to the same thing at the same time.

If you've more than one child to keep amused then a box on the back seat with a few toys in it is worth packing. We'd take the favourite dolls and dolly clothes, plasticine or play dough in an ice-cream tub (they use the lid as a mat to work on), Lego or Magnetix, and even colouring things. We are fortunate that neither of our kids gets car sick, so they'll also read, play with computer consoles and listen to music for hours without complaint.

We know we are fortunate they are good travellers, but we also work on preparing them several days ahead, letting them know what the routine will be and what to expect from each part of the journey—'There'll be lots of open countryside and not much else so we'll need to grab the loo when there is one', or 'We'll be going on lots of windy roads for part of the way tomorrow, but we'll go slow and have the windows down so we get lots of fresh air. When we get to the end of the bends we'll stop at the first nice place and kick the ball around for a while.'

After one marathon 10-hour drive that had us adults shaking and whimpering with tiredness, our young son said brightly, 'I thought you said it would be a long drive today.' We nearly wept with gratitude.

Travelling games—you know them: 'Animal, vegetable, mineral?', 'I spy with my little eye...', the alphabet game ... We've played them all and it's part of being a kid, isn't it—sitting in the back of the car playing 'I spy with my little eye' and having your parents give sarcastic answers. When you tire of those, try a visual scavenger hunt, with points issued to the first person to spot each thing—10 points for a moving train, 50 points for a giant vegetable statue, 30 points for a milk tanker ... We also do prediction. What time does each person think we'll arrive? What will the outside temperature be? How many kilometres will we be up to by the end of the day? Give points for the closest answer, total up the points on a daily basis and keep track for an overall winner at the end of the trip. Prizes might be in order!

After one marathon 10-hour drive that had us adults shaking and whimpering with tiredness, our young son said brightly, 'I thought you said

it would be a long drive today.' We nearly wept with gratitude.

9. **Take lots of breaks:** little kids are guaranteed to sleep for at least part of the journey; determine to keep going until they wake if possible, then stop frequently. We found it better to reward their good behaviour with a quick stop at a playground, park or short beach break rather than with lollies or ice cream. A new playground is always a source of great excitement. Pack active amusements: a 10-minute kick around with a football while you are taking a break will wake everyone up and provide a mental break in the journey. Think skateboard, tennis ball, Frisbee or skipping rope.

We bought our kids cheap folding scooters—they took up very little room in our very loaded car and were great when we were travelling. Wherever we stopped the kids loved to jump out of the car and scoot up and down the main street while we gassed up or bought a coffee. The scooters also provided a diversion when we were staying in motels because the kids could scoot in the driveway.

When you've sat in the car all day it's good to get out and get active—everyone will be less cranky. If you don't pack stuff for them to do they'll get out of the car and go and sit in front of the motel's TV.

Choose toys and activities that are easy to pack away, and that won't break anyone's heart if they go astray en route.

10. **Day bags:** packing a day bag for each person, with their own snacks, water bottle, chewing gum, jumper, music, toys and amusements for the journey, can save you an awful lot of neck-wrenching turning around and passing things over to the back seat. If the kids have their own bag they are less likely to have reasons to squabble and they can get their own snacks when they fancy them. We found it helpful to have a box of amusement stuff on the back seat for them to access as well as what was in their day bags. The box also formed a physical barrier between them, so they couldn't invade each other's space and indulge in pinching, slapping and kicking each other without being really conspicuous.

Chapter 8

OUT AND ABOUT ON THE CHEAP

Down-shifting, or radically down-scaling your career and lifestyle, has become a trend these days. In our case, we only ever intended it to be a short-term thing; if we'd known that we'd still be living this way 15 years later I'd never have believed it. Living well on less remains a lifestyle long after it ceases to be a necessity because once you recognise the many ways you can live well on less it's hard to go back.

The choices you make in this lifestyle journey are entirely individual and I am certainly not suggesting we all move to the country and live off the land. Having said that, we have good friends who have chosen to move to a rural area or a small town because it can be a cheaper lifestyle in many ways. Without the temptation of shopping malls, cafés, restaurants and movie theatres they believe they live a simpler, more meaningful and less stressful life. Their kids grow up with less pressure to have the latest styles, and there's the chance to own their own home in the future because housing is cheaper. With more space for growing food they can be more self-sufficient, and they can enjoy outdoorsy hobbies and close-knit country schools. Good for them, I say. But I'm a city girl.

I love the city and enjoy all that it has to offer, from a stimulating arts scene to a world-class hospital, as well as loads to do all year round, much of which is free.

I like that we are able to travel in any direction and get out of the city if we choose to, but it suits us and our interests to do our 'live well spend less' lifestyle in suburbia.

Regardless of where you live, transport, parking and food all cost, and even being at work all day can rack up expenses. Some of those costs are unavoidable, and others can be offset along the way by making savings in different areas.

It all comes down to choices again. I choose not to buy lunch when we're at the mall, so I can buy the kids an ice cream when we go to the beach.

I don't buy cake in cafés, so that we can go out to a restaurant once in a while ... I make lunches for the whole family every school and working day of the year. It's better for our budget and it's better for the planet.

In Mumbai, India, every working day, approximately 170,000 tiffin boxes are delivered by tiffin wallahs to office workers all over the city. The boxes are collected from individual homes, and delivered to the owners at their places of work in time for lunch.

It all comes down to choices again. I choose not to buy lunch when we're at the mall, so I can buy the kids an ice cream when we go to the beach.

The tiffin box is a stack of round metal tins that clip together and contain a selection of home-made foods—bread or rice in one, dhal or meat and gravy in another, vegetables in another—fresh from the recipient's own kitchen, 170,000 of them a day! The chap who runs the tiffin-wallah service says that food made at their own homes is more suited to the digestion of the office workers. I'd have to agree with that. I adore Indian food. I love that the company that delivers the tiffin boxes in Mumbai employs 5000 illiterate workers to deliver them. And I think it's brilliant that the service is so efficient that in 140 years they've only had a hundred-odd complaints. So impressive is this operation that the tiffin wallahs have featured in *Forbes* magazine. They don't even use a computer.

Even more marvellous are some of the other things they don't use: styrofoam, plastic cling-wrap, plastic bottles, cellophane and foil wrappers, plastic cutlery or plates, paper napkins, paper boxes, Tetra-Pak or any of the other inorganic or non-renewable paraphernalia that is so much a part of western lunch culture.

Using the following tips when you are out and about will save you significant amounts of money every day, and will substantially reduce waste and its impact on the environment, so it's a win-win all round:

- Take a small coffee plunger and some ground coffee to work—no more buying daily expensive frothy coffees unless there is a reason, such as taking out a client or meeting your partner for coffee.

> I like to meet Rich in town for a catch-up during the week from time to time. I save us loads of money by being smart with our grocery spending every week. Because I do that, I can spend a little on a coffee out from time to time, despite our limited resources. If we didn't have any surplus money we would forgo the coffee, meet in a park, and I'd bring a picnic like I did when the kids were babies and we were meeting Daddy for lunch in the city.

- Don't buy snacks at work, and stay away from the cafeteria and sandwich vendor. Keep a snack-box for yourself in the office, stocked with lovely home-made stuff or long-lasting snack foods. What did you think all those drawers in your desk were for?
- Take a packed lunch from home every day. A home-made sandwich takes only minutes to make and can cost less than a dollar. You'll be lucky to find any sort of sandwich in the city for under $5. It's not rocket science, it's home economics. Save here so you can spend somewhere else. A couple of months of home-made lunches will save you

enough for a nice restaurant dinner out. Which would you rather have? If you feel self-concious about bringing a packed lunch get over it. If you are the only one bringing lunch from home and your workmates raise their eyebrows, tell them you have a complicated medical disorder, or that you are avoiding using non-renewable or non-biodegradable disposal utensils and food receptacles, or other 'green speak', to get them off your case. But you shouldn't have to justify yourself. Making good choices is something to be proud of, and I guarantee you'll find others will follow your lead. You'll be able to munch your lunch in comfort on a cold winter day, while your colleagues turn up their collars and head out into the wind and rain foraging for food from some greasy-spoon café, or coughing up for an overpriced panini from the pretentious place that thinks a flat toasted sandwich is 'gormay' food.

- Think tiffin—get a thermos and keep soups and stews deliciously hot when you are away from kitchen facilities. A good thermos will last decades, it's well worth the investment for a hot lunch in cold weather, and brilliant when you want a coffee at the beach or while listening to jazz in the park. A thermos of soup is a great school lunch, and really cheap picnic food in cooler weather. A thermos of hot chocolate for after sports in the wintertime, or following a blustery walk along the beach, will make you a legend with the kids.

- Keep a selection of easy-to-grab snacks in the pantry and freezer. Muffins, scones, muesli bars and suchlike are quick to make, yield a lot and freeze well. Make sure you grab something before you dash out, otherwise you'll get hungry and end up buying food that will cost you a lot and won't be as nice as what you could have made yourself for substantially less.
- Keep some long-lasting snacks in an airtight container in the car —rice crackers, nuts and raisins, pretzels. These are not for mindless munching while you drive, but so you can be spontaneous. You can stop at the park or go for a stroll on the beach and not need to buy something because you're all hungry.
- Prepare a 'day bag' before you leave the house with the kids so you don't get caught out with thirsty, hungry ankle-biters. Put in water bottles, basic sandwiches that don't need refrigeration, and whatever else is to hand—fruit, baking, crackers, raisins. With the best will in the world, plans can change at a moment's notice. A flat tyre, traffic drama or simply bumping into friends and staying longer than you intended are all potential disasters if you've got hungry, whiny kids, and a lovely day can rapidly spiral out of control. The 'day bag' is the answer; you can even train the kids to help prepare it so you never leave the house without one. It will save you a lot of money over the years, as well as a lot of stress. Get in the habit of saying

before you leave: 'Got my keys, got my phone, got the day bag? Right everyone, time to go.'

- Have a coffee fix before you leave the house. With the required amount of caffeine coursing through your veins you won't crave a bought one every time you pass a café.
- Meet friends at home or at a park rather than at the coffee shop. I've mentioned this before, but I can't stress enough what a relief it is not to have to agonise over whether you should or shouldn't have something simply because everyone else is. Arrange social get-togethers that you can afford. Picnics are cheap and fun, and can be both elegant and affordable. A brunch barbecue at the beach is much less expensive than a night-time barbecue as you won't be expected to serve oodles of steak and chicken. Try french toast and barbecued bananas with maple syrup...
- Be sensible about takeaways—fish and chips on the beach on a summer evening is a memorable and relatively inexpensive treat. Takeaways every week because you can't be fagged cooking is an extravagance that your waistline won't thank you for. Keep treats as treats.
- Make sure the kids eat something before you go out, and don't wait for them to get to the hungry, grizzly stage. If you top them up before hunger pangs kick in, you can prevent tantalising smells doing their evil work. Ever walked past a fast-food joint when your tummy is rumbling? It's just cruel,

and it's enough to make a grown-up want to burst into tears, let alone the littlies.

- A lot of venues charge a fortune for food and drinks simply because they can—once they have you through their doors you are a captive market. Theme parks and movie theatres in particular spring to mind. The mark-up they put on rubbishy food and drinks is astronomical.

> We take our own popcorn and drinks to the movies and have never been challenged on this by the staff. Our kids feel no shame about taking their own snacks as they know how ridiculously high the prices are at the cinema. We've also taken packed lunches to theme parks, hot pools, etc. There is likely to be signage that says only food purchased on the premises may be consumed there, so as law-abiding citizens we get our hands stamped at the gate so we can leave and return. That means we can pop out to the car (whereupon we scoff our lunches) and re-enter the park or pools to enjoy the rest of our day and maybe buy a treat later.

- Fairs, markets and festivals fall into the 'treat' category for us, so we allow money for a treat if we're going to a market or fair. If the kids want to spend their pocket money on candyfloss, that's fine, and it won't be the end of the world if they're hungry later because the day bag is packed and there are some snacks in the car for the journey home if we need them. We take cash so it's easy for everyone to keep track of what they've spent. It's also important for kids to spend their own money, learn to keep track of it, count their change and even get ripped off occasionally—we all probably remember buying some piece of tat as kids that broke before we even got it home.

Chapter 9

CELEBRATE WITH STYLE

I love a party—any excuse to put on a party frock and pop some champagne corks is just fine by me. In fact, I think it's really important to celebrate and have things to look forward to.

I know birthdays, New Year and Christmas fill some people with a sense of dread, because they've no sooner paid off the credit card from last year's big blow-out than there seems to be another expensive event on the horizon. Without a doubt, worry about debt and expense is a sure way to pour cold water on the festivities.

We've used a bit of native cunning and over the years managed to celebrate every birthday and Christmas with pomp and presents and excitement and meaning even in our most frugal phases.

When you ask people about their most memorable Christmas or birthday, what they tend to talk about is the people—people they love, people they've lost, people they never want to see again as long as they live ... People, not presents, is what we remember. Don't get me wrong, I love to give and receive gifts, and they're an important part of the way our family celebrates, but they're not THE most important part, for anyone.

Can you even remember what you got for Christmas the year before last? What about your 17th birthday? What you may recall are the traditions that were part of your family culture. You might know that your grandparents were present, the cake came after the meal, the gifts were opened at a certain time ... because that's the way it was done every time in your family. Those traditions form a framework that actually takes a lot of the stress and pressure out of celebrations because you don't have to reinvent every little detail every year—some things simply don't change.

We've used a bit of native cunning and over the years managed to celebrate every birthday and Christmas with pomp and presents and excitement and meaning even in our most frugal phases.

Family traditions also create a framework for expectation and excitement, driving our kids to the very brink of madness with anticipation. They know what is going to happen and they know it's going to be good, and they get very, very excited. The framework of their family life is more important to them than the presents and I love that. And it is just a framework—the basics might stay the same, but the details do change from year to year.

Christmas

Kiwis may not deck the halls with boughs of holly but the New Zealand Christmas is every bit as traditional as that of our European counterparts; it's just that our traditions vary hugely from family to family depending on their culture of origin.

My Danish friends drink Gløgg every Christmas Eve, a fiendishly alcoholic mulled wine, then they merrily dance around their Christmas tree just as they did back in Denmark. The Poms, God bless them, still think having Christmas in the southern hemisphere is unnatural, and because it's summer they stoically picnic regardless of the fact that it's frequently humid, drizzly and blowing a gale. Kiwis tend to favour more informal family gatherings, multiple dessert choices, and might even fire up the barbecue.

Your Christmas event may not look very traditional, but traditions are simply things that become more significant and meaningful the more times you do them, and feasting has to be one of the best traditions in any culture. It's also one of the most expensive, especially at Christmas when budgets are stretched to the maximum.

As a culture we are inclined to shop for Christmas as though we are preparing for a siege, so if you want keep it under control, take the time to identify the things that are the most important to your particular celebration. Some thoughtful analysis can leave you with more cash for the traditions that are really precious to you and help avoid unnecessary excess.

Don't get me wrong—I love excess! I'm a greedy girl, and one of the joys of Christmas for me is the anticipation of eating so much I have to lie down for a little while. But I'll enjoy my post-prandial nap on Christmas Day much more if I know I'm not still going to be paying it off in February.

- Have you planned the main course meal for the big day?
- How much will it cost?
- What do you need to order ahead?
- Discuss the menu with your extended family (or just move overseas and let them fight it out among themselves...)
- If you are hosting the big day, let others know in plenty of time what you want them to bring—don't leave it to the last minute or you'll end up doing it all—remember last year?
- Will you have enough room in the fridge? Cook, cover, chill or get ill!
- Don't forget the drinks!

Christmas gift giving

A word to new parents and grandparents—it's very tempting when the children are little to make or buy a big 'Santa Sack' to hold all their presents. The type of presents suitable for small children tend to be large and relatively inexpensive, so the Santa Sack may seem like a good idea at the time. However, the presents of teenagers are minute, and excruciatingly expensive, and if they're used to having a Santa Sack they'll still expect a bulging stocking or sack every year. This will become increasingly challenging to fulfil, with the result that the Santa Sack may end up having to have an 'accident' that renders it beyond repair before it sends you to the poorhouse.

A modest-sized Christmas stocking will be easier to fill whatever the children's ages and stages, and bulkier presents can go under the tree. We don't want Santa getting the credit for all those things anyway! We want our kids to know from an early age that we carefully chose their gifts.

We enjoyed the magical years when our kids believed in the big guy with the beard, and we played along with the myth, putting out reindeer food and the works. But even then, Santa only got credit for the stocking stuff. We always gave the kids their main prezzie 'with love from Mum and Dad'.

Stocking stuffers

Think about including some items that are useful, and inexpensive, along with the treats. We always include some summer survival stuff that is appropriate to the age of the recipient.

- For littlies you might include a tub of play dough, sand or bath toys, chocolate money, a couple of new T-shirts, a squirt gun, a comic or game, a flash new toothbrush and some bubble mixture or pavement chalk...

- For older ones we include things like a roll-on sunblock or lip balm, a new beach towel or sunglasses, tennis or cricket balls, candy, a box of their favourite treat cereal, some of their favourite fizzy drink, multipacks of new undies, or a pair of togs, a petrol voucher or a movie pass...

At some point in the last hundred years 'Giving' came to mean 'Spending'. If you want to give well and spend less there are lots of presents that you can make for people of all ages that will be precious and memorable, and if done well, every bit as good as a bought one. Here are just a few ideas:

No cost

- **Journey vouchers:** I will drive you to a mate's place and collect you...
- **Get out of trouble free vouchers:** may not be used in situations that are life-threatening or morally threatening, but ideal for teenagers who may have neglected to do their chores, mind their manners or hand in their homework...
- **Leisure vouchers:** soak in the bath, have a lie-in, a cuppa in bed, or sleep till you wake...
- **Babysitting vouchers:** this is a good way teens or grandparents can do something nice for the younger members of the family...
- **Housework vouchers:** cook's night off, I'll be your lawn lackey, oven-clean voucher...
- **Back or foot rub:** do unto others as you would have them do unto you...

- **Tactless remark patch:** you may want to include one in your husband's Christmas stocking; it works like the get out of trouble free voucher for teenagers—does not apply in situations that are life-threatening or morally threatening.

Low cost for preschool and primary children

- **Dress-up bag:** an old suitcase, stocked with cast-off accessories and clothing such as handbags, old high-heeled shoes, necklaces, hats, scarves, lacy stuff from op shops, fairy skirts, an eye patch and pirate gear from the $2 Shop.
- **My school years album:** decorate a ring binder and fill it with sleeves or envelopes to contain examples of each year's work as a record of the school years. Each year's certificates, school photos, etc. get stashed in the appropriate envelope. You can add bits to be filled in for each year, such as: My best friend this year was ... My height on my birthday was ... My favourite food is ... This year I learned to ... The highlight of my year was ... My favourite movie was ... All the stuff that they think they'll remember forever at the time. When they're teenagers they'll get a great laugh from looking back, and they'll remember so much more.
- **Music compilation CD:** make a compilation of some of their favourite music for in the car or just having a dance around at home. This is something that older siblings can easily make for little broth-

ers and sisters, and the littlies will think it's cool because it came from their older brother or sister.

- **Super-capes:** use red, blue, purple or black lining fabric, which is very cheap. Cut a large rectangle, no longer than neck to knees (any longer and it will get tangled in the wheels of the trike), edge all sides with a sewing machine then fold over at one end to make a channel. Stitch, then feed wide elastic (suitable for waistbands) through the channel, checking that it is long enough to go over a head easily and fit loosely around the neck. Stitch each end of the channel to the elastic to stop the cape sliding around the elastic. The wide elastic doesn't scratch like Velcro, doesn't need to be tied by a grown-up and won't choke anyone—they'll be able to put it on and take it off easily and safely without assistance.
- **Fairy skirts:** gather layers of tulle or curtain net onto a wide elastic waistband, and decorate with sequins, ribbons, artificial flowers and anything sparkly.
- **Crafty creations kit:** stock a plastic fishing tackle box with plasticine, glitter, glue sticks, stickers, coloured paper, confetti, scissors and other crafty stuff.
- **Celebration setting:** for each child choose a beautiful dinner plate, napkin ring and twirly glass and place in a decorated box for them, with instructions to use the 'Celebration Setting' when a special achievement has been made, a certificate has been

issued, or on their birthdays and as an acknowledgement of extra effort or exceptional behaviour. The celebration setting turns any meal into a 'special dinner' without the cook having to alter the menu. Make sure there is a candle on the table, as they'll expect to blow it out, and we recommend choosing a long-stemmed glass—it's more 'grown up'.

- **Make and bakes:** pre-measure ingredients for a baking project, include simple instructions and a piece of appropriate cooking equipment such as their own cookie cutters or wooden spoon, and package in a bag or tin with the recipe attached. Try recipes such as gingerbread men, chocolate chippies or brownies. If doing a cake, wrap the ingredients in cellophane in the appropriate-sized cake tin.
- **Fabric painting project:** supply fabric paints and a couple of plain pillow slips or T-shirts for them to decorate and use. You could also include some sequins or other decorative bits.
- **Junior chef set:** make or buy an apron—a child-sized apron is really handy to have and thermal fabric works well for home-made ones, as the rubbery backing keeps paint or chocolate from soaking through into clothing. Make a basic pattern, check the size, and edge with bias binding. Supply cookie cutters and recipe.
- **Little artist's frame:** a wooden picture frame with a removable back, into which current artwork can

be placed and exhibited. Include Blu-tack for positioning the artwork, and a wire or cord to hang it on their wall.

- **Growing gardener:** small gardening gloves, trowel and seeds, packaged in a terracotta pot. Choose seeds that are super-easy to grow, such as sunflowers, sweet peas or something edible.
- **Knit-wit kit:** big fat knitting needles, some fat wool, a cotton reel with four small nails tacked into the top and a crochet hook (for French knitting). Print simple instructions off the internet and include a challenge. If you've knitted a scarf x cm long by June, I'll treat you to a...
- **Little builder:** small tack hammer, tacks and a small saw in a tool box (the tools can be added to over subsequent years), and a sack of wood offcuts for hammering and nailing into.
- **Knight's shield:** cut a shield shape out of a piece of lightweight, flat board (discarded cupboard doors would do) using a jigsaw. Attach a handle to one side (door handles that screw in at either end are ideal) and paint a crest on the front in waterproof paint. You can find loads of heraldic crests online or at the library, or just paint in a basic checkerboard or contrasting wide strips and put a sticker in the middle—a lion or a lightning bolt...

Low cost for teens

- **Funky cushion kit:** supply fake fur or satin, cut to a simple shape—a crown, heart, star, etc.—include stuffing, stick-on jewels and fabric glue or glitter paint. All they have to do is stitch around the edges, turn it right side out, stuff it, and then they can decorate it.

- **Summer survival kit for guys:** sunblock stick, cheap beach towel, cricket ball, whistle, energy drink, instant noodles or other awful but loved-by-teens snack food, batteries, movie voucher, spray deodorant...
- **Summer survival kit for girls:** sunblock stick, lip gloss or cheapie make-up item, sarong, beads, spray deodorant, energy drink, magazine or DVD voucher...
- **Disposable camera**
- **Super-soaker water gun**
- **Kick back and relax pack:** for girls include a voucher to hire a DVD, a magazine, a nail polish, two drinks, two packs of microwave popcorn and permission to have a friend around. For boys include a voucher to hire a game, two drinks, candy, snacks, and a voucher to have a friend around.

Gifts for men

- **Kick back and relax pack:** heart attack-inducing salty snacks, magazine, favourite alcoholic beverage (e.g. a can of imported beer) and a voucher for peace and quiet or to enjoy watching the match without interruption.
- **Cook-up kit:** purchase inexpensive barbecue tools or kitchen utensils; present them in a simple and stylish package with a home-made spice rub, a marinade and some home-made barbecue sauce.

- **Never miss a date again calendar:** a calendar for the year with all the important dates marked in—anniversaries, birthdays, holidays—so he can hang it where he will be reminded and not have to pretend he knows them off by heart.
- **Home-made compilation CD:** this is one the teenagers can make for dads, uncles or grandparents; burn a selection of his favourite music onto a CD for his car.
- **Brother-in-law baking:** my sister started this tradition; each of her brothers-in-law receives a tin of a very special treat that she makes only for them.

Gifts for women

- **Découpage pinboard:** buy a simple corkboard with a wooden frame, cut out decorative images to decorate the frame, then coat with clear varnish—I have one decorated with hundreds of coffee cups—very me.
- **Bath indulgence:** a mini bottle of champagne or favourite wine, bath salts or candles, glossy magazine, chocolate, and an hour or so to indulge without any hammering on the door or floating their boats in your bathwater...
- **Home-made lotions and potions:** bath bombs, hand and foot creams, tub teas, massage oils, bath crystals ... recipes abound, ingredients are cheap and the results are luxurious.

- **Hand-printed table linen:** buy plain calico napkins and stamp or stencil them—keep the pattern simple.
- **Tea break:** a pretty mug or a vintage cup and saucer with a pack of tea in complementary colours.
- **Vouchers:** romantic interlude vouchers—for couples—massage, cuddles, candle-lit dinner...

Batch baking

Every year I resolve to be one of those people who shop in the January sales to put things away for the following Christmas—it's a really good idea, I simply can't manage to do it myself. So instead of blowing the budget in a frenzy of panic buying, 'batch baking' has become a regular part of my Christmas preparations—the selection of handmade festive goodies, mixed and matched, wrapped and beribboned, that we will give as gifts, stocking fillers and thank-yous at Christmas time.

I really like wrapping presents; it's my favourite part of Christmas (except for the overeating, of course). The way a gift looks is important to me.

Wrapping might mean finding funky little boxes, bags or tins in which to present our goodies, or it might mean making gift bags and tags, or recycling wrappings and ribbons. To feel good about giving something we have made, it has to look as good as a bought one—presentation and packaging are part of the cost. Seeing those satisfying rows of batch baking smartly presented makes me feel clever and resourceful—a welcome change from my usual messily disorganised status—and home baking is accepted currency in most social situations. Turn up unannounced but armed with something you whipped up earlier and you are virtually guaranteed a warm welcome.

While I am frequently attracted to new recipes for flash or exotic treats I have to be realistic about the cost of ingredients. I try to choose recipes that aren't cost prohibitive and yield a generous amount. Batch baking must also keep well, as it may not be eaten till after Christmas.

Wrap it up

- For presentation ideas check out the Warehouse, emporiums and $2 Shops for sets of tins, baskets or trays, flax boxes or Polynesian-style kete bags.
- Small plates or platters are a good option, as are boxes and bags.
- Tins can be sprayed different colours if need be, or choose canisters, jars and containers that can be useful in the pantry—practical rather than decorative. Glass preserving jars will show off your efforts to great effect as well as keeping them fresh. Airtightness is important—tie cellophane around foods before placing them in bags or boxes.
- Keep an eye out for little decorations—ornaments that can adorn a gift and be hung on the tree the

following year add an element of permanence to an edible gift. Include an ingredient listing (in case of allergies) and a 'Best before' date so your efforts get enjoyed while they're at their best.

Birthdays

Party tricks

One of my friends realised recently that by the time the youngest of her five children was 15 and no longer expected a big fuss on his birthday she would have conducted 75 birthday parties!

The challenge for parents is to make each one special and memorable for the birthday child, and not go bankrupt in the process. The trend for production-line parties at party venues continues to grow, and although it is an easy option, it can also be an expensive one. We have opted for 'at-home parties' and like to think we do a pretty good one, considering we only have 28 under our belts so far.

Financial constraints mean that most of our party fare is home-made, and as such pretty economical, and it's probably reasonably healthy too compared to party-venue-type food—but please don't tell the kids!

To ensure you don't overspend, advance planning is essential. In the weeks leading up to the party buy one thing a week at the supermarket—a bag of chips or bottle of fizzy, cheerios, sweeties or balloons.

Keep the food simple and colourful. What you serve will depend on the ages of the children—popcorn, sandwiches, cupcakes, fruit kebabs and sausage rolls for a 'little people' party; for teenagers we lean towards platters of nachos and spicy potato wedges, and make a tower out of individual muffin-sized cakes so everyone gets their own ... But take some time to decorate—presentation is everything.

For littlies you want them to eat at the table, so decorate their place settings; for bigger kids, outside is ideal if possible—try a bonfire or brazier, string up the Christmas lights and stock up on ear plugs.

Whatever their age, presentation is everything!

Tips for a great party at home

- Don't allow behaviour that you wouldn't usually tolerate, such as jumping on furniture, walking around with food, etc. It's much better to prevent expensive accidents than be left clearing up after them.
- Ice is fascinating to kids; keep a jug of water with loads of ice on the table. Leftover ice from a bag can be used for a big game of trying to stick ice down each other's backs later.
- State a 'pick up' time on the invitations or you may find yourself acting as an unwitting babysitter.

- Over-prepare activities; better to run out of time than have a pack of bored kids prowling through the house.
- Movies are a cheap entertainment option for sleepovers and at-home parties. If you are showing movies, state the title and rating on the invite; just because your child likes scary or spooky doesn't mean everyone does.
- If teens are selecting the movies check them out first. The website www.screenit.com gives an outline of the content as well as the rating—and double-check they got the movies they said they were getting!

FYI

A teen we know was invited to a girl's birthday party. They screened a really nasty movie, and rather than watch something he wasn't comfortable with, our friend amused himself on the computer in another room. While this was not a problem, the birthday girl's father couldn't quite believe that a boy wouldn't like the yucky stuff and proceeded to tease and humiliate the young chap, calling him names and generally being a git.

Teenage girls seem to have a voracious appetite for horror flicks, not always shared by the lads.

If teens are selecting the movies check them out first. The website www.screenit.com gives an outline of the content as well as the rating—and double-check they got the movies they said they were getting!

> We've let the kids go and collect the movies, only to have them come home with a completely different selection than what was previously agreed upon, usually because one person says, 'Oh, I've seen that; it's so lame—we should get "xyz".' None of the others are brave enough to say they're not supposed to, or they don't want to watch 'xyz'. Then you have to try and sort out a complicated negotiation with the kids, and the DVD rental place, and it's really a bore. Set the rules first: 'If you don't come back with the movies we agreed on, we reserve the right not to screen them.'

For the under-10s

- Presentation is as important as the food itself. Having balloons, plates and cups at each place-setting is a good start; you could add place cards, or a named party bag if you are doing party bags.
- Encourage them to keep all their stuff together: 'Why don't you put your prize in your party bag—it's by your glass, at your place at the table—then you'll know where to find it at home-time.' Can save a lot of tears, probably yours!

- Name each child's cup, or use distinctive stickers or twirly straws they can take away with them. They're much more likely to keep track of their own if their name is on it. If not, you'll go through a million cups and end up with half the glasses broken too.
- Set a specific time for food so they don't drift back and forward eating only the treats. Some kids think it's fine to jump up and down on your couch with a fistful of bright orange cheesy snacks in one hand and fizzy drink in the other. Rather than being a tyrant and chasing them around telling them off every two minutes, explain that we will all go to the table and have our treats after we've finished the games. They'll need to eat then because we'll be clearing the table afterwards to make room for the cake/craft activity...
- Expect them to sit at the table or on a rug to eat, or you'll be vacuuming sprinkles out of the carpet long after the kids have moved out. Just keep reminding them to sit down while people are eating. If one wanders off you'll lose them all in no time. It's like dealing with sheep—keep 'em in a bunch and bark occasionally if one breaks away.
- Plan to serve savoury food first.
- If you're doing a birthday cake it's a good idea to save it to just before leaving time as many of the kids will prefer to take a piece home to enjoy after all the excitement.

For the over-10s

- Food theme parties work well. Pizza is a good option—make a batch of dough, roll it out into discs and have each child top their own with a selection of prepared toppings. Write each child's name on a piece of baking paper and place their pizza below their name before baking, as they'll look much the same when cooked. Gluten-free kids can use a prepared gluten-free base. Dairy-free kids can use soy mozzarella on their pizza; it has a good cheesy flavour and no dairy products.
- My 13-year-old son recently had spaghetti bolognaise at a friend's party. With loads of garlic bread, it got the big thumbs-up from all the boys.
- Barbecues also work well for teens—at the hot pools, a beach or at home. Keep it really informal and they'll be happy.
- As a change from the ubiquitous DVDs/Xbox/iToy amusements you could stage a water fight, a big game of spotlight in a local park or 'Capture the flag'. Dress-up is often still popular with young teens—try a theme like 'Hairspray' or 'High School Musical', or 'something starting with P'—paparazzi, person, pizza, primate...
- Rope in the relatives and host a car rally or scavenger hunt, or do a bonfire with toasted marshmallows and hot chocolate.

My 13-year-old son recently had spaghetti bolognaise at a friend's party. With loads of garlic bread, it got the big thumbs-up from all the boys.

Avoiding lolly overload

Cheap lollies and mini chocolate bars have become commonplace party-bag fillers and prizes. Here are some non-junk-food options:

- Have the kids make their own party bags. Buy plain lolly bags from a packaging supplier (or, like me, chat up your local dairy owner), and decorate with stickers, stamps, felts, etc. Let them take home the twirly straws from their drinks, a small prize, their piece of cake, a glow stick or two and maybe something they have made (see below).
- Glow sticks—they come in tubes from $2 Shops, with a little bag of connectors. Allow several per child. Teens also like them, they'll just use them differently (sigh).
- Use small cellophane bags, available from Spotlight, with a small treat and attach to a balloon string. Give them out on departure.
- Instead of bags, make leis from long strips of tulle folded in half lengthwise and sewn to make long tubes. Slip small items such as a lollipop, bouncy ball, balloon, party popper, etc. into each tube and then divide it into sections using

brightly coloured curling ribbon. When each tube is filled, sew the ends together to form a lei.

- Instead of a party bag, give each child a single 'special treat'. Try decorated cookies—bake them on Popsicle sticks, ice and decorate, then wrap in cellophane with twirly ribbons—and maybe a tiny toy, and let each child select one from the 'bouquet' to take home.
- Buy a multipack and split it for party bags: body glitter, bubble bath, sparkly nail polish, lip gloss, hair ties, soaps, bath crayons, stick-on body jewels, stamps, tattoos, stickers, caps (the noisy exploding kind), funky pencils or rubbers, super-bouncy balls, pavement chalk, bubble mix, party poppers, play dough, marbles, dinosaurs, parachuting soldiers, water bombs ... Check out $2 Shops, emporiums, the Warehouse, etc.
- Include a craft so they can make something to take home.
- Small square canvases for painting or collage are inexpensive at emporiums, or try chocolate-moulding, card-making or scrapbooking a photograph. Jewellery-making is popular with girls and boys, who also might enjoy using fabric paint on cheap pillowslips, having a go at candle-making, or decorating an initial for their bedroom door (letters available at Spotlight)—provide a hot-glue gun, embellishments and a finished example. Just keep it simple!

- For littlies, pre-cut 'crowns' from gold card—provide jewels, tinsel and glitter to decorate.
- Try an egg-and-spoon race using filled water balloons instead of eggs, and encourage any grown-ups to play too—the kids love it when the grown-ups join in. Just don't cry if you don't get a prize!

Many party games also focus on junk food, which is pretty inexpensive but a bit sickening after an hour or two. We changed the famous 'chocolate game' (rolling a six on the dice, putting on the costume and scoffing as much chocolate as you can with a knife and fork before the next six is rolled) into an archaeological dig. We filled the sandpit with buried plastic dinosaurs, the costume was an Action Man flak jacket, boots and hat, and each six allowed you to dig up dinosaurs to take home until someone else in the circle rolled a six...

Cakes

I've made my share of novelty cakes over the years, from the Bananas in Pyjamas cake that had to have just the right shade of blue, to a pirate ship in full sail, a treasure chest, princess, crown and Thomas the tank engine (again that elusive shade of blue!)—hours of back-breaking labour, all happily demolished in under half an hour.

These days I can't always find the time (or energy) for novelty cakes. But cake is still an important part of honouring the birthday child, along with the song and candles, the prezzies and the hip hoorays.

What I am talking about is a 'show stopper' of a cake without the blood, sweat and tears.

These smart and simple 'No Piping Bags Required' decorating ideas are equally handy for anniversaries, adult birthdays and the inevitable work shout:

- **Tins:** for two or more tiers, use a 20-cm cake tin for the bottom. I made a tin for the next tier by cutting down an A10 or catering size tin (ask a local café or retirement home if you can have an empty one from their recycling). Use a hacksaw or tin snips to trim off the top two-thirds, file off any rough edges, and what remains is a perfect little 15-cm, half-size tin.
- **Flowers:** gerberas are funky, bright and last well; white roses and daisies look fine against a chocolate cake but can look 'dirty' against a pale one. Artificial flowers are a good option—try Spotlight and $2 Shops. Buy ready-made icing flowers from cake-decorating shops.
- Arrange **marshmallow** slices in an overlapping circle with a dab of icing and a mini M&M in the centre for cute edible flowers.
- Buy ready-made **Pettinice** icing, available in supermarkets and cake-decorating shops; colour, roll and cut with cake-decorating cutters to make icing flowers and shapes.

- **Lollies:** heaping cascades of jelly beans or Smarties are very effective, the brilliant colours are really attractive and you don't have to worry about the smoothness of your icing. The same goes for chocolate money—just use lots and pile it up—mmmmm. Lollies can also be arranged in easy but funky designs—flowers, swirls, etc.
- **Ribbon:** check out Spotlight or a local emporium for wired ribbon; wind around the rolling pin to shape into soft coils. Organza ribbon is good too—allow for a double layer if using in bands around a cake.
- **Sparkle:** edible glitter and edible paint are easy to apply and go a very long way. Choose a colour that you are likely to reuse.
- **Bought cake:** buy it a day ahead. Older cake is less likely to shed crumbs through the icing as you spread it.
- **Candles:** coloured alphabet candles on short spikes are available in $2 Shops; look for 'Happy Birthday' or 'I love you'.
- **Wired stars or hearts:** use florists' wire and ready-made icing.

Pettinice ready-made mouldable icing is available in supermarkets; it dries to a hard edible finish.

Several days ahead, roll out the icing, colour it with food colouring, and cut out stars or hearts using a cutter. Wind pieces of florists' wire around a pencil to make a spring and insert a wire into each icing shape, then leave in the airing cupboard until completely dry and firm.

The icing can be coloured with food colouring before you cut the shapes, or painted with edible paints when the shapes are dry. Poke the wires into the cake or cupcakes so the shapes appear to 'spring' out of the top.

Chapter 10

FAMILY LIFE

Family life can seem to be expensive from the moment the little blue line appears on the stick and the good news of an imminent arrival starts to sink in. Babies, cots, clothes and car-seats all cost, and we tend to want it all—nice stuff, good schools, extracurricular activities and family holidays. So how do you have a rich family life when you aren't, well, rich?

Peer pressure is a reality just as much for parents as for kids. It affects our decision-making from the earliest days, influencing everything from which brand of nappies to use, to which preschool to send your child to, what extracurricular activities they are involved in, what brand of shoes, bike or bed they might be using, and worst of all, how well they are doing in everything.

We all want the best for our kids, and we don't want them to miss out on anything—we want everything the current age has to offer as well as any advantages we feel we missed out on ourselves.

We all know families who seem to be able to have it all and do it all. Their kids have every imaginable toy, great costumes, the beautiful bedroom and mega birthday parties. The kids attend private schools, have top-flight sports equipment and coaching, overseas holidays, skiing and sailing, voice coaching and dance, camps and riding school ... We hate those people.

OK, we don't actually hate those people, but we don't tend to socialise with them either.

Peer pressure is a reality just as much for parents as for kids.

The easiest way to avoid falling into the 'dissatisfied with your lot' trap is to hang out with people in a similar position to yourself. You'll all benefit from shared resources and moral support. If you spend a lot of time with the 'have it alls' you'll either feel like the poor relation, or become the poor relation by trying to keep up, paying for stuff you can't afford and your kids probably won't thank you for.

It gets harder for the kids themselves, too, if the young 'uns they are seeing and socialising with have much more 'stuff' than them. I'm not suggesting that you ditch all your wealthy friends and relations, but as many of our long-term friendships are actually formed when our children are little you can choose to be around people with similar priorities to you. During those early years there are so many shared experiences and similar challenges that people bond over baby buggies and in antenatal coffee groups—they share sleep-deprivation stories and teething traumas, the terrible twos and terrifying teens.

You might not be able to choose your family but you can choose your friends. So choose to spend time with the people you get on with the best, and who are at a similar stage in life to you.

The easiest way to avoid falling into the 'dissatisfied with your lot' trap is to hang out with people in a similar position to yourself.

When we were looking for a playgroup/child-care option for our daughter, a friend with much more money than us recommended the exclusive and expensive preschool she was using. Explaining that I couldn't afford it was awkward and embarrassing, and I felt I was somehow failing my daughter by not giving her 'the best'. Someone else told me about the local community crèche which operated on a coin donation, piece of fruit and parent-help system. It was within walking distance of home, great fun, and a perfect and much less expensive solution to my childcare needs. Despite that, I still felt like I'd let my baby down whenever my friend talked about her preschool—silly, I know, but honest.

It's easier to keep yourself on the financial straight and narrow in these situations if you follow these suggestions:

- Buying baby gear: buy second-hand—you're mad if you don't. Bassinets, changing tables, high-chairs, baths and all the other little baby paraphernalia are useful, but only for a short time. If you go looking at new stuff I guarantee you'll fall in love with something expensive.
- Ask around, go to recycle shops and check out the auction websites. You'll still find stuff you love, but you'll pay a lot less for it.
- Many people are happy to lend equipment when they are between babies; they'll need it back when number two is due, but in the meantime you have the use of it.
- Clothing is another area where second-hand can be brilliant. You won't want to buy all your baby's clothes second-hand, I'm sure, but kidswear recycle shops and online auctions can be a brilliant source of inexpensive designer clothing.
- Outlet shops are also a cheaper way to get the kinds of clothes you might like. Find out where they are—just don't go crazy. Kids outgrow their clothes long before they wear them out. Say yes to hand-medowns too; it may not be a garment you would have chosen but it's one you don't have to buy; it'll be fine for the sandpit or helping in the garden, or passing on to someone else who might love it.

- The same principles apply to school uniforms—HORRIBLY expensive and outgrown often before the year is out. Can you buy second-hand basics like shorts or skirts? Then you only have to get new shirts. With boys' uniform socks costing as much as $15 per pair it pays to take care of the uniform. If you do have to purchase a new uniform, you may well be able to sell it on when your child no longer needs it, and spare some other hapless parent facing financial ruin in the uniform shop. Word of mouth and asking around can be your greatest asset here.

> I bought beautiful little designer dresses and shoes for my daughter from recycle shops and sold them the following season when she'd outgrown them. I'd wash and press the clothes carefully and take them in on hangers. In some cases I sold garments for more than I originally paid for them.

Learn to ask around

There are all sorts of situations where a bit of 'inside knowledge' can save you money. Friends, schools, libraries, community notice-boards etc. are all good sources of information. The following popular activities can be expensive, but by asking around you can often find a cheaper option that's just as good.

Swimming lessons

Baby swimming lessons have become really popular. Don't be sucked into thinking you can drown-proof a baby, the lessons won't teach your baby to 'swim', but they are fun for parents and babies—check out the local pool for cheap daytime 'mums and bubs' sessions. Swimming lessons are frequently offered through public pools for both adults and kids, and will be cheaper than a swim school. Some swim clubs also offer 'entry level' swim training; depending on the club it can be very reasonable or very expensive.

Music lessons

Private music lessons are not the only option for budding musicians. Independent 'music schools' operate on Saturday mornings in many local schools. Based in, but independent of, the local school, the lessons are taught in groups, using the various classrooms for differing age levels and instruments. Instrument hire is usually available and kids can often learn more than one instrument. Classes are usually pretty small, and the range of instruments limited to those that can be taught in a group setting.

Itinerant music teachers work in many schools; the lessons are more expensive than the Saturday music school but are likely to be 'one to one' lessons during school time so you aren't tearing around dropping kids off and picking them up. The student will be taken out of class to attend the lesson, but this is done with the cooperation of the class teacher. You can expect your child to progress through grades and have the opportunity to take exams.

Music lessons may eventually pay for themselves, as young musicians can earn quite surprising amounts of money busking, scratching out a few Christmas carols at the weekend market. More competent teenage musicians with a few musical grades under their belts can give music lessons to beginners. And when they get to the 'starting a band' stage they may get paying gigs, although bands often cost more than they earn in equipment for the first few years.

Sports

A wide variety of sports are offered in schools, but to compete competitively it is usual to join a club. Clubs are pretty good at self-promotion in the run-up to a season. Billboards appear near athletics, football, netball and rugby clubs, with contact phone numbers etc. For more specific clubs—harriers, cross-country, triathlon, gymnastics, etc.—we've found we needed to ask around. Some clubs will do a grading session, others will grade during the season.

You will be expected to pay your subscription (subs) for the season or year, and will need to pay for most or all of the uniform or equipment. If a club has sponsorship, shirts may be provided, but things like football boots, hockey pads, mouth guards, running shoes, etc. are all ongoing expenses, and there will always be some kid with better gear than yours.

Some sports are much more expensive than others—we had a competitive swimming child and faced the ongoing cost of replacing swimsuits and goggles, fins and caps, all of which deteriorate because of the chlorine. Plus there were the subs, meet fees, club nights and pressure to buy other club gear—robes, jumpers, etc.—and attend club weekends and camps, all of which made it an extremely expensive venture. Not to mention the training six times a week, and in some cases twice a day. It was a huge commitment, not just financially.

Sailing, triathlon, windsurfing, skiing and other individual sports are equally expensive and require regular gear replacement due to intensive wear and tear, but they are tremendously rewarding.

In some cases the biggest expense may be in travel and time—rowing, for example, or surf lifesaving.

Team sports such as netball, football, hockey, water polo, rowing, cricket, etc. are less expensive at entry level. But once your young sportsperson starts competing at a serious level, be prepared to pay for travel, more uniforms and accommodation.

Triathlon involves three separate sports, each with its own specialised equipment and training—wind trainers, bikes, wetsuits and running shoes, training schedules and coaching ... When our young swimmer branched into triathlon we found she was financially disadvantaged—without the $4000 bike and the wetsuit she couldn't perform as well as those with all the top gear. Fortunately for us she was less inclined to pursue a sporting career at that stage and more interested in lip gloss and hairstyles—whew!

We've never regretted a penny spent on sports for the kids—they're fit, confident and have learnt to be team players who can work with others and push themselves when necessary—and they used up lots of energy which might otherwise have been expended in door slamming and answering back.

Buying the gear

Most clubs sell gear—our swim club had cheap 'sample' swimsuits for sale at a set price, as well as their compulsory club suits for competitions (very expensive). Most people took advantage of the cheap suits for training, and people would spread the word when there was a good sale on.

Remember, one person's idea of a bargain and another's can be completely different—ask around. We found out about a sports wholesaler from whom we were able to buy other compulsory equipment significantly cheaper. It may also be possible to buy second-hand gear through the club or by word of mouth.

It really helps to get to know other families who also have to watch what they spend, and share resources, car pool, etc.

Online auction sites are fantastic for buying sports gear, new or used. If branded stuff is important to you, then check out what is available online. It helps to know exactly what you want, know what the regular retail price is and set your budget.

Factor in sales and plan ahead for the following season. Sports retailers often have a pre-season sale, and your club may arrange a discount with a preferred retailer.

For littlies, who will have outgrown their gear or changed their minds about their sporting career by the end of the season, it pays not to commit to top-of-the-range equipment.

Playing for the school is often a cheaper way of trialling a sport first off than joining a club. A sport enthusiast may well do both, although the real competition will probably happen at club level.

Teens who are accomplished in their sport can earn money or have their club fees subsidised by assisting junior divisions in coaching or refereeing. Ask about work opportunities at the club.

It really helps to get to know other families who also have to watch what they spend, and share resources, car pool, etc.

Drama and dance

Drama and dance will have many of the same costs as sporting endeavours—costumes or uniforms, shoes and training fees, plus exams.

Cheaper after-school and community programmes are a good starting point, as you might discover your prima ballerina suddenly wants to swap dance for karate when you've just shelled out for a complete set of costumes.

Dance shoes and costumes can be purchased second-hand. When it's likely they'll be outgrown within a few months it makes sense.

Some dance schools require the students to have a complete kit before they start, others may be happy to allow a grace period while you acquire the necessary kit—ballet, for example, may require ballet shoes, tap shoes, leotards, tights, wraps, skirts, character costumes, hair accessories and music to practise to. Jazz or hip hop may only require shoes and shorts or a leotard.

Drama and dance are likely to involve recitals and performances for which you may be expected to buy or sell tickets, the proceeds of which pay for venue hire, programmes, etc. You may also have to hire or sew costumes, help with make-up and attend rehearsals, all of which will cost in time and money. Ask up-front so you know what you are letting yourself in for and can budget as required.

Free activities

Weekends and holidays are a precious part of family life. If you live in the city, check out the local and central councils for free family programmes. Some will operate seasonally, others year round.

We made great use of a programme called 'Families in parks' which moved from local park to local park—dropping off all sorts of outdoor play equipment for parents and their kids to have fun with from 5–7pm during the daylight-saving period of the year. We also frequented free concerts, teddy bears' picnics, kite days, 'Live' days, Highland days, Easter egg hunts, beach digs, and Navy open days.

We clambered over ships, trains, planes and horse-drawn carts at various museum-type attractions. And when all else failed there was the zoo.

We loved the zoo and got great value from our 'Friends of the zoo' passes, which gave us unlimited entry for one year. Young kids often get more from frequent short visits than an annual extended one. The same goes for the museum. An hour looking at the volcano exhibit or marvelling at the dinosaurs then a big game of chasey in the park outside was much more popular than three hours shuffling around every exhibit.

We also made a lot of our own fun; gathering a band of like-minded families together we formed 'future friends', an informal group of parents and young children. We'd meet up at a park or arrange a get-together in someone's garden, with everyone contributing food and activities that parents and kids could do together. We had craft days, box-sliding afternoons, sing-alongs with home-made instruments, outings on ferries and trains, and lots of themed 'at home' events that people could invite their friends and neighbours to as well. Sometimes 70 or more parents and kids would get together to picnic and play.

Easy outdoor activities for families and groups

Free

- **Box-sliding:** you'll need a steep grassy hill and some large cardboard boxes. The big ones that appliances come in are brilliant for tumbling down hills inside; when they disintegrate use the large flat pieces like a sled. Head first, sitting up or one behind the other, race each other downhill and on the run back up. Pack drinks, sunblock, the camera and snacks—it's physical, hungry- and thirsty-making play.
- **Bat down brunch:** during summer getting out before the sun really heats up is a good idea. Plan a picnic brunch in a park with a coinoperated barbecue. Make up a batch of french toast mix in a plastic tub and grab a bottle of maple syrup. Buy a couple of cheap baguettes on the way to the park. Slice them up, dunk in the eggy mixture and cook on the barbecue; serve with maple syrup and coffee or juice. Take a bat and ball and play 'Bat down'. Pitch the ball to the batter. When the ball is struck the batter lies the bat down on the grass;

the fielders must roll the ball across the grass to strike the bat to get the batter out.

- **Water-bomb warfare:** water bombs (balloons) are inexpensive and terrific fun. Arm each team with a few water pistols and a bucket of filled water bombs and even empty squeezy detergent bottles and have a full-on water fight.
- **Pirate picnic:** we held one of these events with friends on a very windy beach in full pirate regalia. We played silly games, did a treasure hunt and had a picnic (and gathered quite a crowd of onlookers too). You'll need to be completely without shame, kitted out from the dressup bag with pirate clothes and eye patches, and have some treasure (we used a little chest of chocolate money) to bury and hunt for.
- **Camp out:** pitch the tent in the garden and sleep in it with the kids—you'll need insect repellent, a torch, story books and a midnight feast.
- **Mexican fiesta:** invite friends to bring kid-friendly Mexican-type food, make a piñata in advance, and do craft activities—we made those pretty woollen decorations of coloured yarn wound in and around two crossed sticks.
- **Water slide:** you'll need a long sheet of heavy polythene, garden hose and washing-up liquid ... Position in a grassy area, apply a little detergent and turn on the hose or sprinkler. Run and slide.
- **Night-time games:** Spotlight and 'Capture the flag' are great fun for outdoors in the garden at

night-time—rules vary, so play your own favourite version or Google if you can't rememeber (or agree on) the rules.

- **Check out your local parks:** we bought a book that rated every park in our city—we chose those with loos and playgrounds or loos and ducks or loos and a bike track...
- **Teddy bears' picnic:** stories, cookies, and a blanket in the park...

Cheap

- **Jellification:** jelly crystals are cheap—make loads of jelly and do jelly games and activities—suck the jelly up the straw, eat the lolly off the top of the bowl of jelly, run an obstacle course holding a plate of jelly, throw the jelly at the target ... we did this with around 40 kids in teams (each with its own colour of jelly). We finished with a massive jelly fight—fantastic fun, needed to hose the house down afterwards though.
- **Camping:** once you've got a basic camping kit together, a night or two at a campsite is great fun and not too arduous with littlies, as there are loos and showers.
- **Agricultural shows:** so much to see—baby animals, giant pumpkins, wood-chopping, sheep-shearing. Take your own food and drink, so you can spend your pocket money on a treat.
- **Live days:** museums and pioneer or heritage villages host 'Live' days several times a year. Volunteers will be in costume, and there will be demon-

strations—blacksmiths, horses and carts, scary Victorian schoolmasters, and often steam trains or other exciting, noisy stuff. You may also see 're-enactors' acting out a battle from a particular period. There are medieval or Viking re-enactors as well as First and Second World War enthusiasts complete with 'grenades and bullets'. You'll pay to get in, and expect it to be crowded—'Live' days are well publicised and popular.

CONCLUSION

Ask the average person what their dream is and they are likely to reply, A first division win in the big national lottery. Make me rich, rich, rich!

My family and I live in New Zealand, and because of that alone I figure I've already won the lottery.

I wasn't born into a civil war, or a famine or a drought.

Cholera, TB and malaria are practically unknown here, and I can drink the water with confidence.

Both my children, regardless of gender will be immunised and educated just as I have been and the generation before me.

My daughter can choose to dress, work, and marry or not according to her own wishes, and my son will never be forced in fear of his life to become a child soldier, slave, prostitute or beggar.

We can worship and vote as we please, hold radical opinions and read whatever we want.

These freedoms are riches, most of which we take for granted. But for much of the world's population, these are freedoms they can only dream about. By world standards I (and you) am rich beyond their wildest imaginings.

Most of us would agree that money doesn't buy happiness, but we would also agree that financial freedom is a big step on the way: less stress + less pressure = more leisure.

My hope is that, like us, you will find that living well has more to do with realising what you do have than what you don't, and using your freedom and making your choices well. Popular American minister Rick Warren once said, 'Your response to your circumstances can make you Bitter or Better.' I think there is a lot of truth in that.

Making the decision to live well and spend less is a nail in the coffin for bitter and a giant leap towards better. Better for our families, better for our environment, better for our health. So you better get started, there's never been a better time or place to live well and spend less.

Printed in Dunstable, United Kingdom

91226154R00127